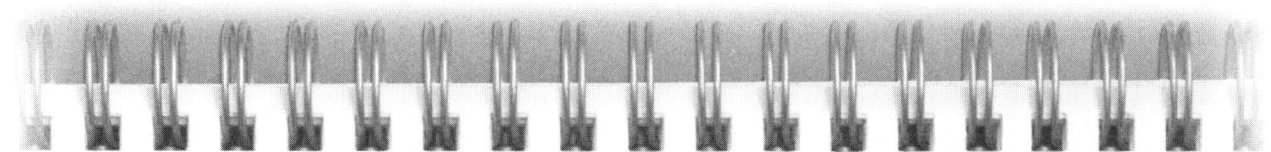

Interactive Notebooks

Grade 4

Credits

Content Editor: Elise Craver

Visit *carsondellosa.com* for correlations to Common Core, state, national, and Canadian provincial standards.

Carson-Dellosa Publishing, LLC
PO Box 35665
Greensboro, NC 27425 USA
carsondellosa.com

© 2015, Carson-Dellosa Publishing, LLC. The purchase of this material entitles the buyer to reproduce worksheets and activities for classroom use only—not for commercial resale. Reproduction of these materials for an entire school or district is prohibited. No part of this book may be reproduced (except as noted above), stored in a retrieval system, or transmitted in any form or by any means (mechanically, electronically, recording, etc.) without the prior written consent of Carson-Dellosa Publishing, LLC.

Printed in the USA • All rights reserved

978-1-4838-2465-9
02-191157784

Table of Contents

What Are Interactive Notebooks? 3
Getting Started 4
What Type of Notebook Should I Use? 5
How to Organize an Interactive Notebook . . . 6
Planning for the Year 8
Managing Interactive Notebooks
in the Classroom 10
Interactive Notebook Grading Rubric 11

Number and Operations in Base Ten

Place Value 12
Number Forms 14
Comparing and Ordering Numbers 16
Rounding Numbers 18
Adding and Subtracting Whole Numbers . .20
Factors .22
Multiples 24
Multiplying Large Numbers 26
Multiplying Two-Digit Numbers 28
Dividing Large Numbers 30

Number and Operations—Fractions

Equivalent Fractions 32
Adding and Subtracting Mixed Numbers . .34
Multiplying Fractions and Whole Numbers .36
Relating Fractions and Decimals 38
Comparing and Ordering Decimals 40
Adding and Subtracting Decimals 42

Operations and Algebraic Thinking

Is It Reasonable? 44
Patterns 46
Unknown Numbers 48

Measurement, Data, and Probability

Converting Measurements 50
Elapsed Time 52
Area and Perimeter 54
Line Plots 56
Probability 58

Geometry

Points, Lines, and Rays 60
Parallel and Perpendicular Lines 62
Introduction to Angles 64
Measuring and Drawing Angles 66
Finding Unknown Angle Measures 68
Classifying Polygons 70
Symmetry 72
Transformations 74
The Coordinate Plane 76

Reproducibles

Tabs 78
KWL Chart 79
Pockets 80
Shutter Folds 83
Flap Books and Flaps 85
Petal Folds 90
Accordian Folds 92
Clamshell Fold 94
Puzzle Pieces 95
Flip Book 96

What Are Interactive Notebooks?

Interactive notebooks are a unique form of note taking. Teachers guide students through creating pages of notes on new topics. Instead of being in the traditional linear, handwritten format, notes are colorful and spread across the pages. Notes also often include drawings, diagrams, and 3-D elements to make the material understandable and relevant. Students are encouraged to complete their notebook pages in ways that make sense to them. With this personalization, no two pages are exactly the same.

Because of their creative nature, interactive notebooks allow students to be active participants in their own learning. Teachers can easily differentiate pages to address the levels and needs of each learner. The notebooks are arranged sequentially, and students can create tables of contents as they create pages, making it simple for students to use their notebooks for reference throughout the year. The interactive, easily personalized format makes interactive notebooks ideal for engaging students in learning new concepts.

Using interactive notebooks can take as much or as little time as you like. Students will initially take longer to create pages but will get faster as they become familiar with the process of creating pages. You may choose to only create a notebook page as a class at the beginning of each unit, or you may choose to create a new page for each topic within a unit. You can decide what works best for your students and schedule.

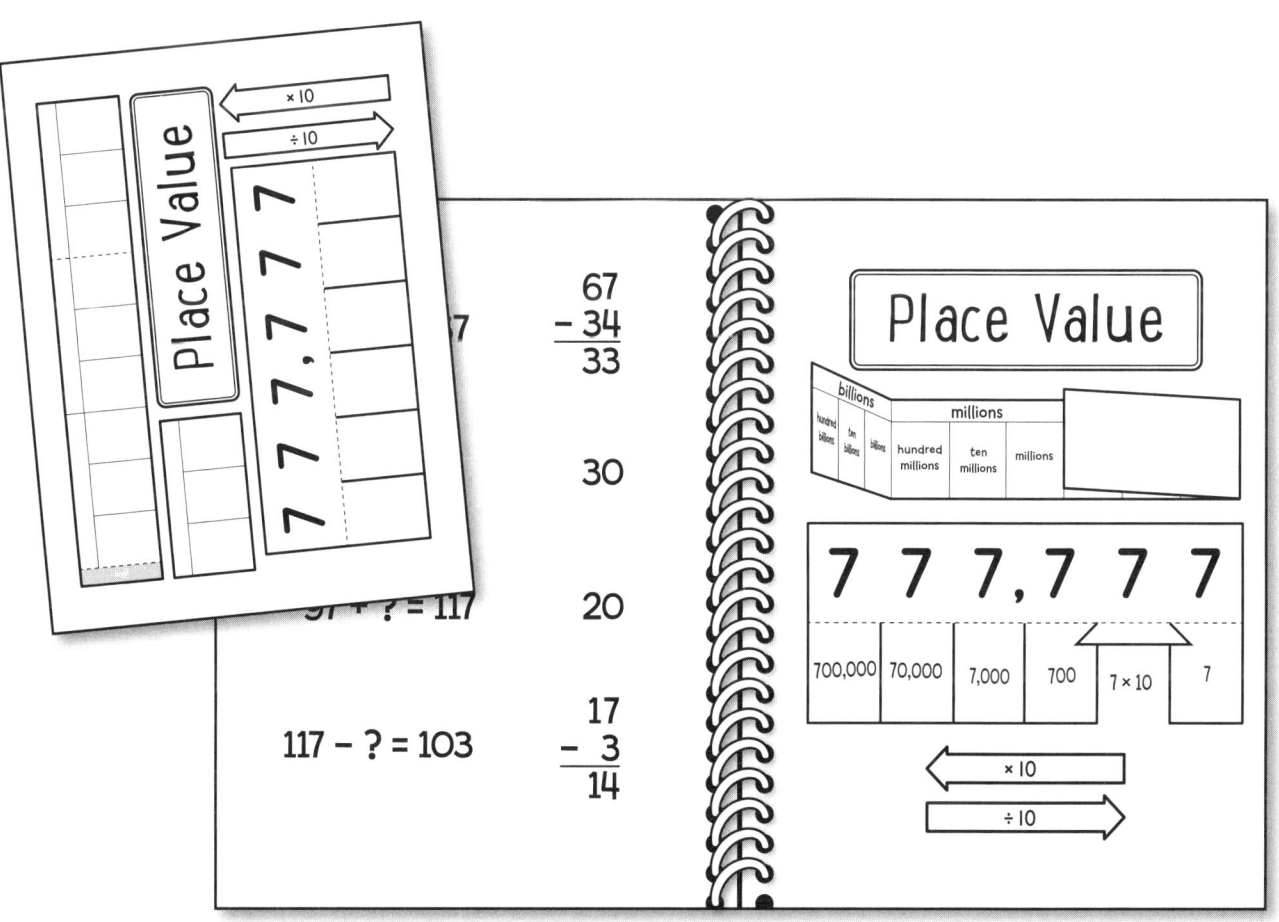

A student's interactive notebook for a place value page

Getting Started

You can start using interactive notebooks at any point in the school year. Use the following guidelines to help you get started in your classroom. (For more specific details, management ideas, and tips, see page 10.)

1. **Plan each notebook.**

    Use the planning template (page 9) to lay out a general plan for the topics you plan to cover in each notebook for the year.

2. **Choose a notebook type.**

    Interactive notebooks are usually either single-subject, spiral-bound notebooks; composition books; or three-ring binders with loose-leaf paper. Each type presents pros and cons. See page 5 for a more in-depth look at each type of notebook.

3. **Allow students to personalize their notebooks.**

    Have students decorate their notebook covers, as well as add their names and subjects. This provides a sense of ownership and emphasizes the personalized nature of the notebooks.

4. **Number the pages and create the table of contents.**

    Have students number the bottom outside corner of each page, front and back. When completing a new page, adding a table of contents entry will be easy. Have students title the first page of each notebook "Table of Contents." Have them leave several blank pages at the front of each notebook for the table of contents. Refer to your general plan for an idea of about how many entries students will be creating.

5. **Start creating pages.**

    Always begin a new page by adding an entry to the table of contents. Create the first notebook pages along with students to model proper format and expectations.

This book contains individual topics for you to introduce. Use the pages in the order that best fits your curriculum. You may also choose to alter the content presented to better match your school's curriculum. The provided lesson plans often do not instruct students to add color. Students should make their own choices about personalizing the content in ways that make sense to them. Encourage students to highlight and color the pages as they desire while creating them.

After introducing topics, you may choose to add more practice pages. Use the reproducibles (pages 78–96) to easily create new notebook pages for practice or to introduce topics not addressed in this book.

Use the grading rubric (page 11) to grade students' interactive notebooks at various points throughout the year. Provide students with copies of the rubric to glue into their notebooks and refer to as they create pages.

What Type of Notebook Should I Use?

Spiral Notebook

The pages in this book are formatted for a standard one-subject notebook.

Pros

- Notebook can be folded in half.
- Page size is larger.
- It is inexpensive.
- It often comes with pockets for storing materials.

Cons

- Pages can easily fall out.
- Spirals can snag or become misshapen.
- Page count and size vary widely.
- It is not as durable as a binder.

Tips

- Encase the spiral in duct tape to make it more durable.
- Keep the notebooks in a central place to prevent them from getting damaged in desks.

Composition Notebook

Pros

- Pages don't easily fall out.
- Page size and page count are standard.
- It is inexpensive.

Cons

- Notebook cannot be folded in half.
- Page size is smaller.
- It is not as durable as a binder.

Tips

- Copy pages meant for standard-sized notebooks at 85 or 90 percent. Test to see which works better for your notebook.

Binder with Loose-Leaf Paper

Pros

- Pages can be easily added, moved, or removed.
- Pages can be removed individually for grading.
- You can add full-page printed handouts.
- It has durable covers.

Cons

- Pages can easily fall out.
- Pages aren't durable.
- It is more expensive than a notebook.
- Students can easily misplace or lose pages.
- Larger size makes it more difficult to store.

Tips

- Provide hole reinforcers for damaged pages.

How to Organize an Interactive Notebook

You may organize an interactive notebook in many different ways. You may choose to organize it by unit and work sequentially through the book. Or, you may choose to create different sections that you will revisit and add to throughout the year. Choose the format that works best for your students and subject.

An interactive notebook includes different types of pages in addition to the pages students create. Non-content pages you may want to add include the following:

Title Page

This page is useful for quickly identifying notebooks. It is especially helpful in classrooms that use multiple interactive notebooks for different subjects. Have students write the subject (such as "Math") on the title page of each interactive notebook. They should also include their full names. You may choose to have them include other information such as the teacher's name, classroom number, or class period.

Table of Contents

The table of contents is an integral part of the interactive notebook. It makes referencing previously created pages quick and easy for students. Make sure that students leave several pages at the beginning of each notebook for a table of contents.

Expectations and Grading Rubric

It is helpful for each student to have a copy of the expectations for creating interactive notebook pages. You may choose to include a list of expectations for parents and students to sign, as well as a grading rubric (page 11).

Unit Title Pages

Consider using a single page at the beginning of each section to separate it. Title the page with the unit name. Add a tab (page 78) to the edge of the page to make it easy to flip to the unit. Add a table of contents for only the pages in that unit.

Glossary

Reserve a six-page section at the back of the notebook where students can create a glossary. Draw a line to split in half the front and back of each page, creating 24 sections. Combine Q and R and Y and Z to fit the entire alphabet. Have students add an entry as each new vocabulary word is introduced.

Formatting Student Notebook Pages

The other major consideration for planning an interactive notebook is how to treat the left and right sides of a notebook spread. Interactive journals are usually viewed with the notebook open flat. This creates a left side and a right side. You have several options for how to treat the two sides of the spread.

Traditionally, the right side is used for the teacher-directed part of the lesson, and the left side is used for students to interact with the lesson content. The lessons in this book use this format. However, you may prefer to switch the order for your class so that the teacher-directed learning is on the left and the student input is on the right.

It can also be important to include standards, learning objectives, or essential questions in interactive notebooks. You may choose to write these on the top-left side of each page before completing the teacher-directed page on the right side. You may also choose to have students include the "Introduction" part of each lesson in that same top-left section. This is the *in, through, out* method. Students enter *in* the lesson on the top left of the page, go *through* the lesson on the right page, and exit *out* of the lesson on the bottom left with a reflection activity.

The following chart details different types of items and activities that you could include on each side.

Left Side — Student Output	Right Side — Teacher-Directed Learning
• learning objectives • essential questions • I Can statements • brainstorming • making connections • summarizing • making conclusions • practice problems • opinions • questions • mnemonics • drawings and diagrams	• vocabulary and definitions • mini-lessons • folding activities • steps in a process • example problems • notes • diagrams • graphic organizers • hints and tips • big ideas

Planning for the Year

Making a general plan for interactive notebooks will help with planning, grading, and testing throughout the year. You do not need to plan every single page, but knowing what topics you will cover and in what order can be helpful in many ways.

Use the Interactive Notebook Plan (page 9) to plan your units and topics and where they should be placed in the notebooks. Remember to include enough pages at the beginning for the non-content pages, such as the title page, table of contents, and grading rubric. You may also want to leave a page at the beginning of each unit to place a mini table of contents for just that section.

In addition, when planning new pages, it can be helpful to sketch the pieces you will need to create. Use the following notebook template and notes to plan new pages.

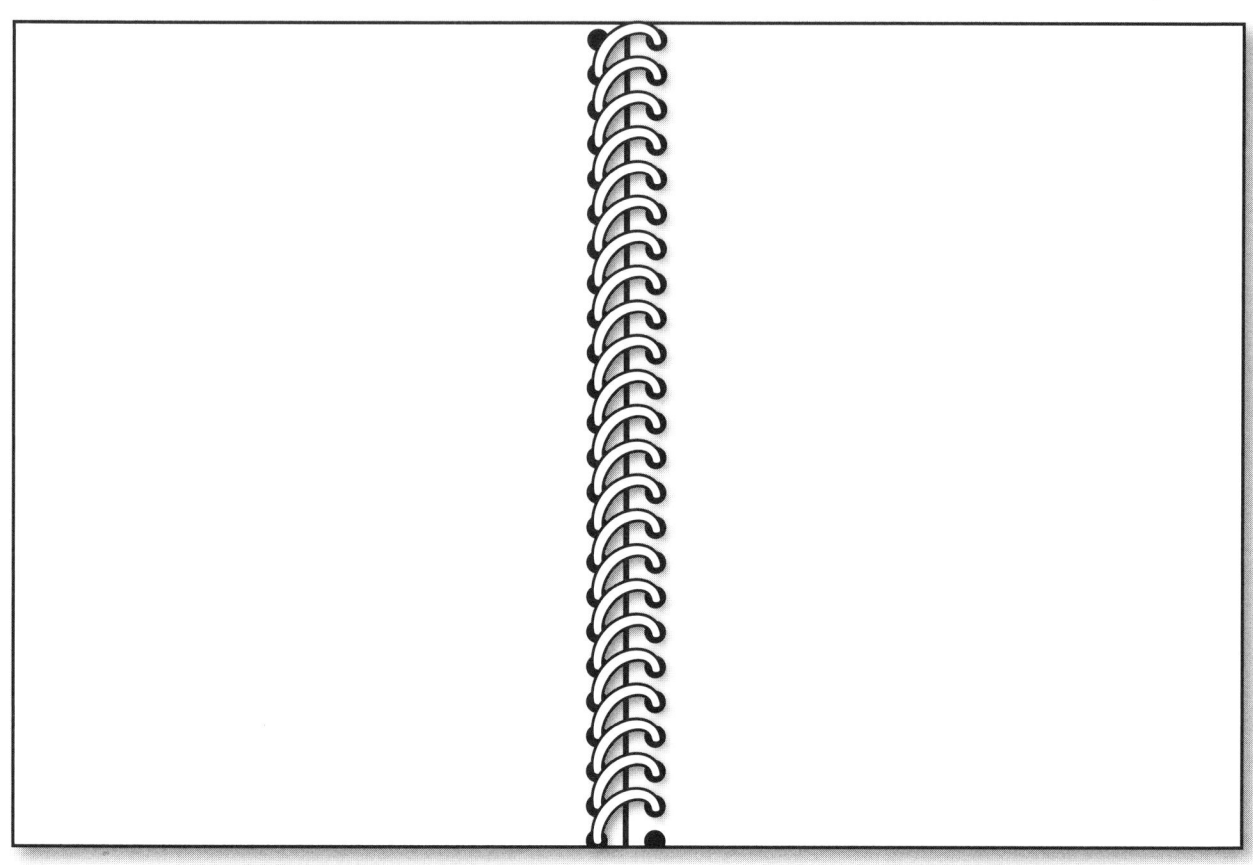

Left Side **Right Side**

Notes

_____

_____

_____

Interactive Notebook Plan

Page	Topic	Page	Topic
1		51	
2		52	
3		53	
4		54	
5		55	
6		56	
7		57	
8		58	
9		59	
10		60	
11		61	
12		62	
13		63	
14		64	
15		65	
16		66	
17		67	
18		68	
19		69	
20		70	
21		71	
22		72	
23		73	
24		74	
25		75	
26		76	
27		77	
28		78	
29		79	
30		80	
31		81	
32		82	
33		83	
34		84	
35		85	
36		86	
37		87	
38		88	
39		89	
40		90	
41		91	
42		92	
43		93	
44		94	
45		95	
46		96	
47		97	
48		98	
49		99	
50		100	

Managing Interactive Notebooks in the Classroom

Working with Younger Students

- Use your yearly plan to preprogram a table of contents that you can copy and give to students to glue into their notebooks, instead of writing individual entries.

- Have assistants or parent volunteers precut pieces.

- Create glue sponges to make gluing easier. Place large sponges in plastic containers with white glue. The sponges will absorb the glue. Students can wipe the backs of pieces across the sponges to apply the glue with less mess.

Creating Notebook Pages

- For storing loose pieces, add a pocket to the inside back cover. Use the envelope pattern (page 81), an envelope, or a resealable plastic bag. Or, tape the bottom and side edges of the two last pages of the notebook together to create a large pocket.

- When writing under flaps, have students trace the outline of each flap so that they can visualize the writing boundary.

- Where the dashed line will be hidden on the inside of the fold, have students first fold the piece in the opposite direction so that they can see the dashed line. Then, students should fold the piece back the other way along the same fold line to create the fold in the correct direction.

- To avoid losing pieces, have students keep all of their scraps on their desks until they have finished each page.

- To contain paper scraps and avoid multiple trips to the trash can, provide small groups with small buckets or tubs.

- For students who run out of room, keep full and half sheets available. Students can glue these to the bottom of the pages and fold them up when not in use.

Dealing with Absences

- Create a model notebook for absent students to reference when they return to school.

- Have students cut a second set of pieces as they work on their own pages.

Using the Notebook

- To organize sections of the notebook, provide each student with a sheet of tabs (page 78).

- To easily find the next blank page, either cut off the top-right corner of each page as it is used or attach a long piece of yarn or ribbon to the back cover to be used as a bookmark.

Interactive Notebook Grading Rubric

4
- _____ Table of contents is complete.
- _____ All notebook pages are included.
- _____ All notebook pages are complete.
- _____ Notebook pages are neat and organized.
- _____ Information is correct.
- _____ Pages show personalization, evidence of learning, and original ideas.

3
- _____ Table of contents is mostly complete.
- _____ One notebook page is missing.
- _____ Notebook pages are mostly complete.
- _____ Notebook pages are mostly neat and organized.
- _____ Information is mostly correct.
- _____ Pages show some personalization, evidence of learning, and original ideas.

2
- _____ Table of contents is missing a few entries.
- _____ A few notebook pages are missing.
- _____ A few notebook pages are incomplete.
- _____ Notebook pages are somewhat messy and unorganized.
- _____ Information has several errors.
- _____ Pages show little personalization, evidence of learning, or original ideas.

1
- _____ Table of contents is incomplete.
- _____ Many notebook pages are missing.
- _____ Many notebook pages are incomplete.
- _____ Notebook pages are too messy and unorganized to use.
- _____ Information is incorrect.
- _____ Pages show no personalization, evidence of learning, or original ideas.

Place Value

Introduction

Review simple place value with students. Distribute index cards with *ones*, *tens*, and *hundreds* written on them. For an irregular number of students, include cards with *thousands* and commas as well. Have students find other students to create the hundreds period in the correct order. Then, once students have correctly demonstrated the hundreds period, ask them to write digits on the back of their index cards to create a number with the value of 4 tens, 7 ones, and 2 hundreds. (Add a thousands value as needed.)

Creating the Notebook Page

Guide students through the following steps to complete the right-hand page in their notebooks.

1. Add a Table of Contents entry for the Place Value pages.

2. Cut out the title and glue it to the top of the page.

3. Cut out the two blank rectangular pieces. Apply glue to the gray glue section and lay the right edge of the smaller piece on top to create a long rectangle with four sections of three.

4. Write the name of each period in the space at the top of each section. Then, write the name of each place in the rectangle below the period name. Fold the two outer sections in on the dashed lines. Apply glue to the back of the millions and thousands section and attach the piece to the page below the title.

5. Cut out the *777,777* piece. Cut on the solid lines to create six flaps. Apply glue to the back of the top section of the piece. Attach it to the page below the place value piece.

6. On the flap below each 7, write the value of the digit. Then, under each flap, write the value of each digit expressed as 7 multiplied by a factor of 10.

7. Cut out the two arrows. Glue the arrows to the page below the *777,777* piece to show the relationship between neighboring place values.

Reflect on Learning

To complete the left-hand page, write five numbers on the board from left to right: 34, 67, 97, 117, and 103. Have students figure out the number needed to add or subtract to the first number to get to the next number in the sequence. After finding all four numbers, students should write an explanation describing how place value can help solve for missing addends and subtrahends.

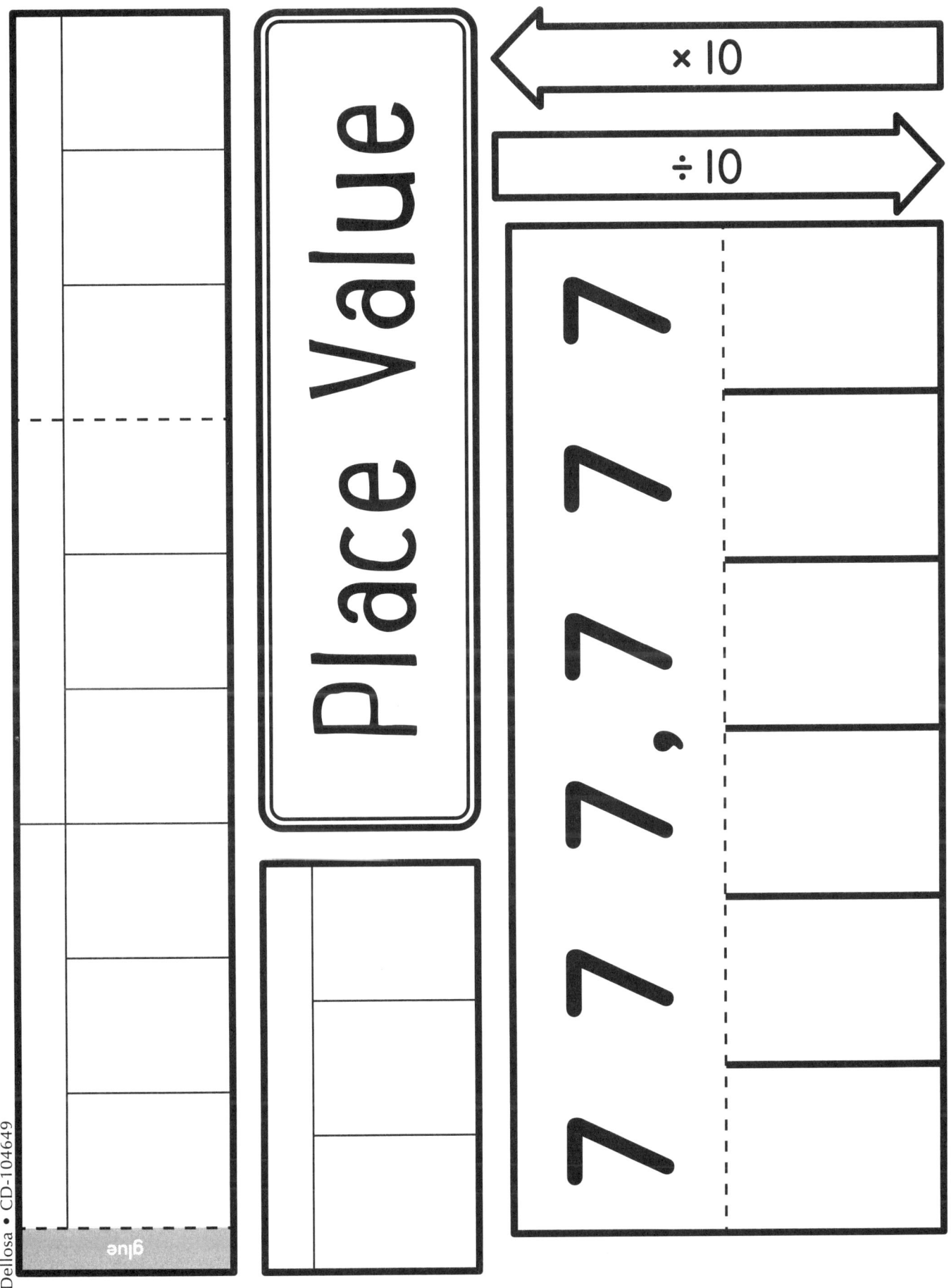

Number Forms

Introduction

Hand one student a piece of paper that says *Clap 2 times*. Hand a different student a piece of paper that says *Clap two times*. Let each student act out the sentence on his paper. Discuss with the class why the students did the same thing, even though their directions were slightly different. Explain that numbers can be written in several forms that all mean the same thing.

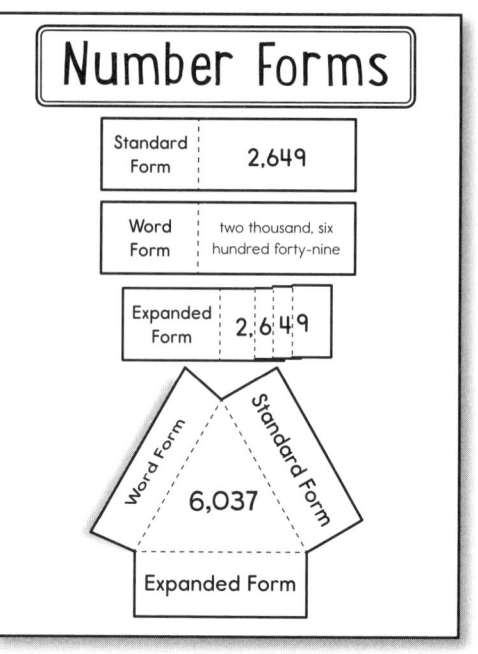

Creating the Notebook Page

Guide students through the following steps to complete the right-hand page in their notebooks.

1. Add a Table of Contents entry for the Number Forms pages.

2. Cut out the title and glue it to the top of the page.

3. Cut out the *Standard Form, Word Form,* and *Expanded Form* rectangles. Fold each piece along the dashed line near the title. Apply glue to the back of the left side of each rectangle and attach it to the page under the title.

4. To complete the *Expanded Form* piece, place the dashed line before the 6 after the comma in 2,000. Press down to flatten. Repeat with the dashed lines before the 4 and the 9, flattening as you go. The piece should show 2,649 when folded and 2,000 + 600 + 40 + 9 when unfolded.

5. Write a short explanation of or helpful hint for each form under the flap formed by each rectangle.

6. Cut out the triangle piece with three flaps. Apply glue to the back of the triangle and attach it to the page. Write any number on the triangle. Write the different forms for that number under each corresponding flap. You may choose to have all students write the same number or allow them to choose their own numbers.

Reflect on Learning

To complete the left-hand page, have students write the three forms for the number 1,700,831 as you say it aloud. Have students describe in their own words how they chose to handle the "missing" numbers in the thousands and ten thousands places.

Number Forms

| Standard Form | 2,649 |

| Word Form | two thousand, six hundred forty-nine |

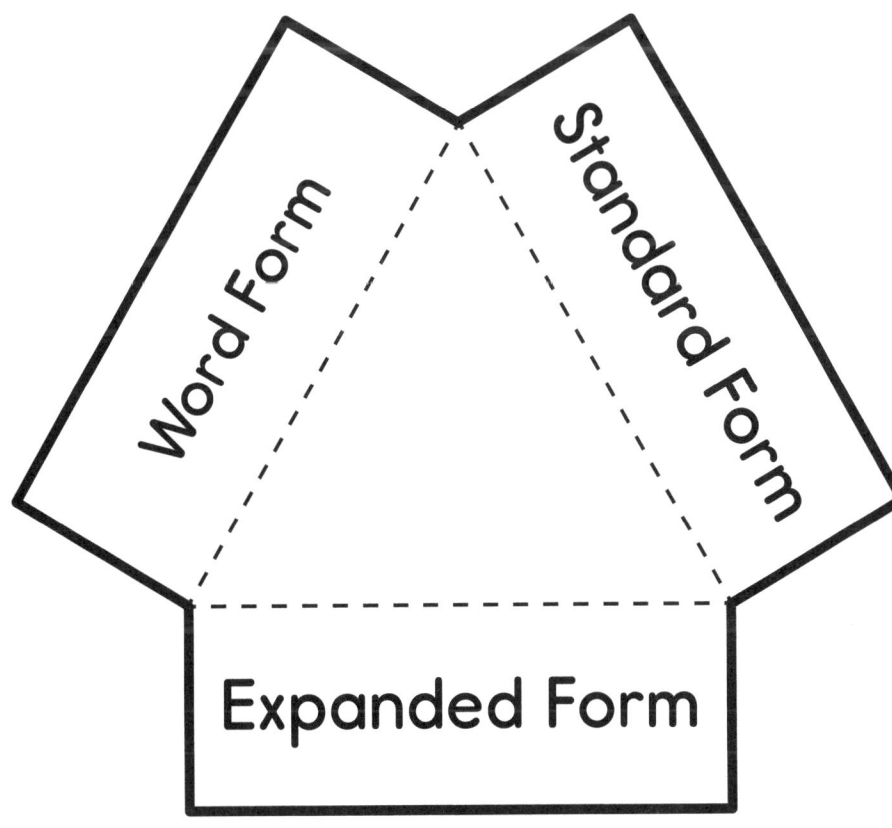

Expanded Form

2,000 + 600 + 40 + 9

Comparing and Ordering Numbers

Introduction

Review the comparison symbols (>, <, and =). Discuss how to "read" a comparison sentence from left to right. Allow students to share their memory devices for greater than and less than, such as thinking of them as alligator mouths, or drawing dots on the ends and vertex of the greater than and less than symbols to show which side has more or less.

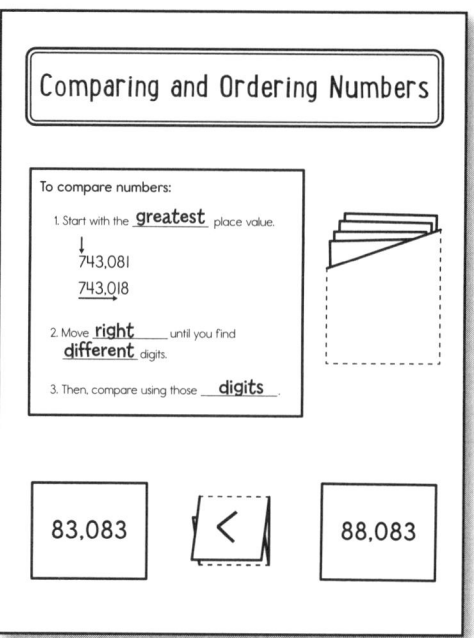

Creating the Notebook Page

Guide students through the following steps to complete the right-hand page in their notebooks.

1. Add a Table of Contents entry for the Comparing and Ordering Numbers pages.

2. Cut out the title and glue it to the top of the page.

3. Cut out the *To compare numbers* piece and glue it to the top left of the page.

4. Complete the steps by filling in the blanks. (1. Start with the **greatest** place value. 2. Move **right** until you find **different** digits. 3. Then, compare using those **digits**.)

5. Cut out the piece with the equal sign. Fold the bottom and top flaps over the equal sign. Apply glue to the back of the middle section. Attach it to the center of the bottom half of the page so that the flaps open up and down.

6. Flip the top flap down and draw a less than symbol (<) on it. Flip the bottom flap up and draw a greater than symbol (>) on it.

7. Cut out the pocket. Fold it in half. Apply glue to the back of the tabs. Fold the tabs around the back to create a pocket. Apply glue to the back of the pocket. Attach it to the page beside the *To compare numbers* piece.

8. Cut out the number cards. Place one card on each side of the symbols piece. Unfold the flaps to create a true number comparison. Or, choose three or more cards to place in order from least to greatest or greatest to least. For more practice, write additional numbers on the backs of the cards. Store the cards in the pocket.

Reflect on Learning

To complete the left-hand page, write 304,627 and 340,627 on the board. Have students describe how the placement of the zero in each number affects the comparison.

Comparing and Ordering Numbers

88,083	83,083	106,761
891,745	891,145	16,761

=

To compare numbers:

1. Start with the _____ place value.

   → 743,081
      743,018 ↑

2. Move _____ digits. _____ until you find _____.

3. Then, compare using those _____.

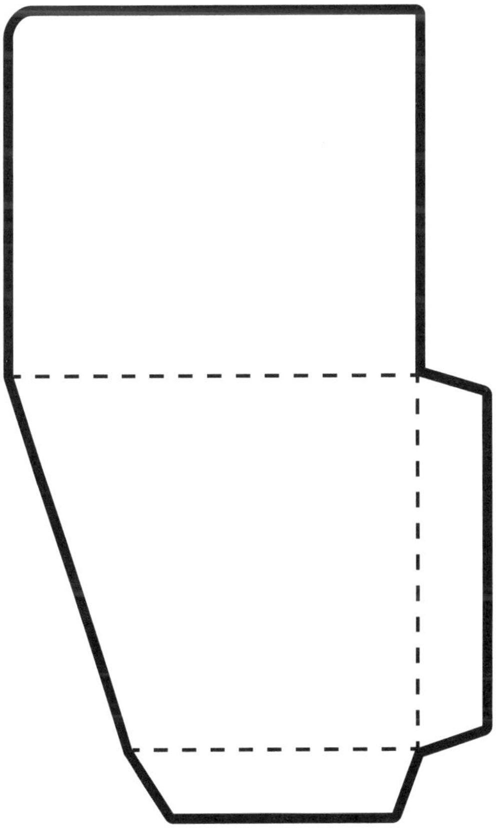

Rounding Numbers

Each student will need a brass paper fastener to complete this page.

Introduction

Write on the board how many students are in the entire school. As a class, discuss situations when someone might need to know the exact number and when someone only needs to know about how many students there are.

Creating the Notebook Page

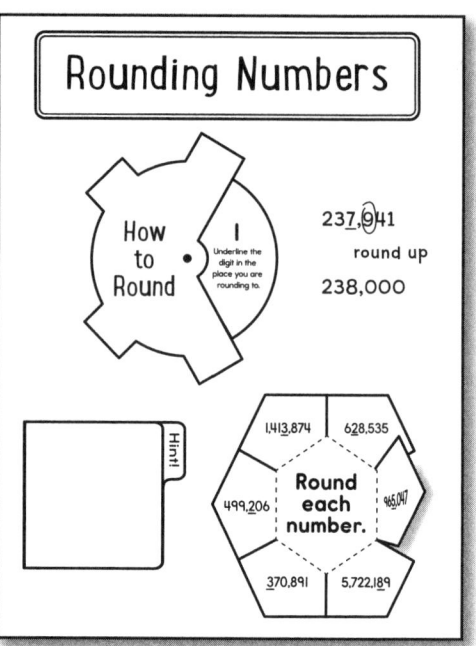

Guide students through the following steps to complete the right-hand page in their notebooks.

1. Add a Table of Contents entry for the Rounding Numbers pages.

2. Cut out the title and glue it to the top of the page.

3. Cut out the circular shapes. Place the *How to Round* piece on top of the circle with step-by-step directions. Push a brass paper fastener through the center dots of the circles to attach them. It may be helpful to create the hole in each piece separately first. Apply glue to the back of the *How to Round* piece tabs and attach it to the left side of the notebook page below the title. The brass paper fastener should not go through the page, and the step-by-step circle should spin freely.

4. Walk through the steps. Write an example to the right of the circle to show each step.

5. Cut out the *Hint!* mini file folder. Fold it in half along the dashed line. Apply glue to the back of the folder and attach it below the *How to Round* circle so that the folder opens to the left.

6. Write the numbers 0 to 9 in the roller coaster cars.

7. Cut out the flower piece. Cut on the solid lines to create six flaps. Apply glue to the back of the hexagon-shaped center and attach it to the right of the *Hint!* folder.

8. Choose a place value to round to for each petal. Underline the digit. Then, write the rounded number under the petal.

Reflect on Learning

To complete the left-hand page, have each student write any 6- or 7-digit number. Then, have students round the numbers to each place value through the hundred thousands or millions. Have students reflect on what they noticed about each rounded number.

Rounding Numbers

How to Round

1. Underline the digit in the place you are rounding to.
2. Look at the number to the right of your underlined number.
3. It remains the same if it is 0, 1, 2, 3, or 4. Round up if it is 5, 6, 7, 8, or 9. Change the digits to the right to zeroes.

Round each number.

- 965,047
- 5,722,189
- 370,891
- 499,206
- 1,413,874
- 628,535

Hint!

original digit → digit +1

Adding and Subtracting Whole Numbers

Introduction

Have students write their birth months and days as numbers. For example, September 9 would be 99, and May 28 would be 528. Then, have students write their four-digit birth years. Students should add the two numbers. Then, students should subtract them.

Creating the Notebook Page

Guide students through the following steps to complete the right-hand page in their notebooks.

1. Add a Table of Contents entry for the Adding and Subtracting Whole Numbers pages.

2. Cut out the title and glue it to the top of the page.

3. Cut out the *Add* and *Subtract* flaps. Fold along the dashed lines. Apply glue to the back of the narrow left and right sections and attach them side by side below the title.

4. On the top of each flap, write words and symbols related to addition or subtraction, such as *+, plus, addend, sum,* etc. Under each flap, write steps in your own words for adding or subtracting numbers. Refer back to the addition and subtraction problems created during the introduction as examples.

5. Cut out the four-flap book. Cut on the solid lines to create four flaps. Apply glue to the back of the center section. Attach it to the bottom of the page.

6. For each flap on the left side, choose two numbers from the center and write them on the top of the flap in an addition sentence. Solve and write the sum under the flap.

7. For each flap on the right side, choose two numbers from the center and write them on the top of the flap in a subtraction sentence. Solve and write the difference under the flap.

Reflect on Learning

To complete the left-hand page, have students write large numbers from their lives such as street address numbers, zip codes, heights, the school's phone number, etc. Then, students should choose two of the numbers to add or subtract. Repeat with different pairings of numbers. Students should have at least two addition and two subtraction sentences.

Adding and Subtracting Whole Numbers

Add

Subtract

346,782

204,302

265,914

813,528

772,018

347,490

245,111

153,058

Factors

Introduction

Play a quick game of Around the World with a set of multiplication flash cards. Have the first two students stand side by side. The first student to correctly answer the problem moves on to challenge the next student in line, and the other student sits in the empty seat. The first student to make it all the way back to her original seat wins. Play until every student has had at least one turn.

Creating the Notebook Page

Guide students through the following steps to complete the right-hand page in their notebooks.

1. Add a Table of Contents entry for the Factors pages.

2. Cut out the title and glue it to the top of the page.

3. Complete the definition of *factors* (numbers **multiplied** together to form a **product**).

4. Write a simple multiplication problem, such as 3 × 6 = 18, below the title. Label the factors and the product.

5. Cut out the four arched shapes with tabs. Apply glue to the gray glue sections. Place the *12* piece on top of the piece with six boxes. Repeat with the *16* piece and the piece with five boxes. Then, glue the back of each pair to the page to create two two-page flap books.

6. Complete the factor rainbow in each flap book by writing the number's factors in the boxes. The factors should be in order from least to greatest and form pairs connected by the lines. Discuss why a factor of 16 doesn't make a pair (4 is multiplied by itself).

7. Cut out the two rectangular pieces. Fold each rectangle on the dashed lines. Fold the piece with the gray glue section so that it is inside the fold. Apply glue to the gray glue section and place the other folded rectangle on top so that the folds meet to create a book with four cascading flaps. Glue the book to the bottom of the notebook page.

8. Label the top of the booklet *Factor Vocabulary*. Then, label the three flaps *Prime Numbers*, *Composite Numbers*, and *Greatest Common Factor*. Complete each page of the book with a definition and an example of each vocabulary term.

Reflect on Learning

To complete the left-hand page, have students complete a Venn diagram to show the factors of 24 and 36. Have them describe in their own words how the Venn diagram relates to the greatest common factor. Then, have students add a third circle to the Venn diagram and add the factors for 42. Students should describe how adding 42 affected the greatest common factor.

Factors

numbers _____ together to form a _____

The factors of **16**

The factors of **12**

Multiples

Introduction

Have students stand in a line. Choose a digit from 0 to 9 to be the "leap" number. Tell students they will be counting by twos (or threes or fives). Starting with the first student in line, each student should say the next number in the sequence, unless it contains the leap number. In that case, the student should say *ribbit*. If a student forgets to say *ribbit*, she should sit down. For example, when counting by threes with a leap number of 2, students should count *3, 6, 9, ribbit, 15*, etc.

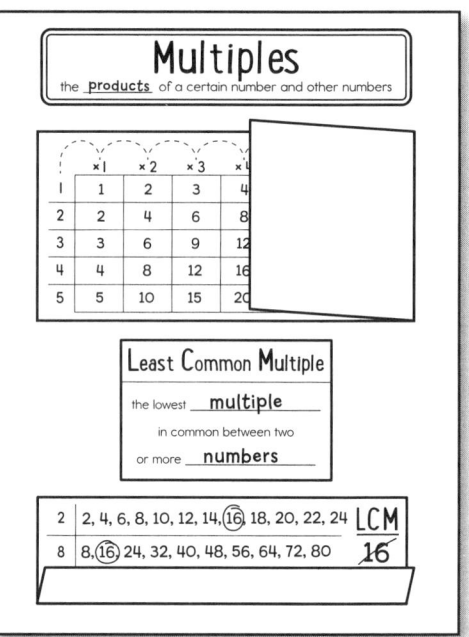

Creating the Notebook Page

Guide students through the following steps to complete the right-hand page in their notebooks.

1. Add a Table of Contents entry for the Multiples pages.

2. Cut out the title and glue it to the top of the page.

3. Complete the definition of *multiples* (the **products** of a certain number and other numbers).

4. Cut out the multiples chart. Fold it on the dashed line on the border between ×7 and ×8 so that it will fit lengthwise on the page.

5. Complete the multiples chart. Apply glue to the back of the largest section to attach it to the page. Discuss how multiples for a number never end because you can always multiply it by the next largest number.

6. Cut out the *Least Common Multiple* piece and glue it below the chart.

7. Complete the definition of *least common multiple* (the lowest **multiple** in common between two or more **numbers**).

8. Cut out the LCM chart. Fold up the bottom tab along the dashed line to cover the *3* row. Apply glue to the back of the top section and attach it to the bottom of the page.

9. Write the first 10 multiples for the numbers 2 and 8. Find and circle the LCM. Then, record the LCM on the chart. Unfold the flap. Write the first 10 multiples for 3. You may have to record more multiples for 2 or 8 to find the new LCM. Record the new LCM.

Reflect on Learning

To complete the left-hand page, have students describe in their own words why the product of two numbers is always a common multiple of those two numbers.

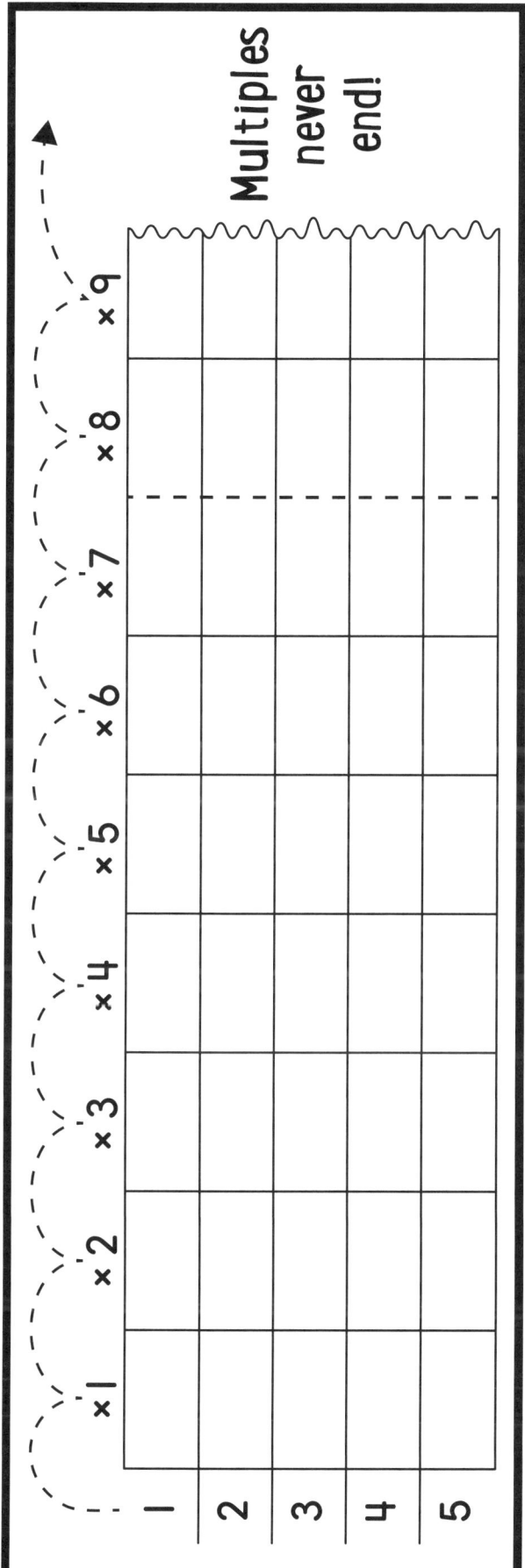

Least Common Multiple

the lowest _____

in common between two

or more _____

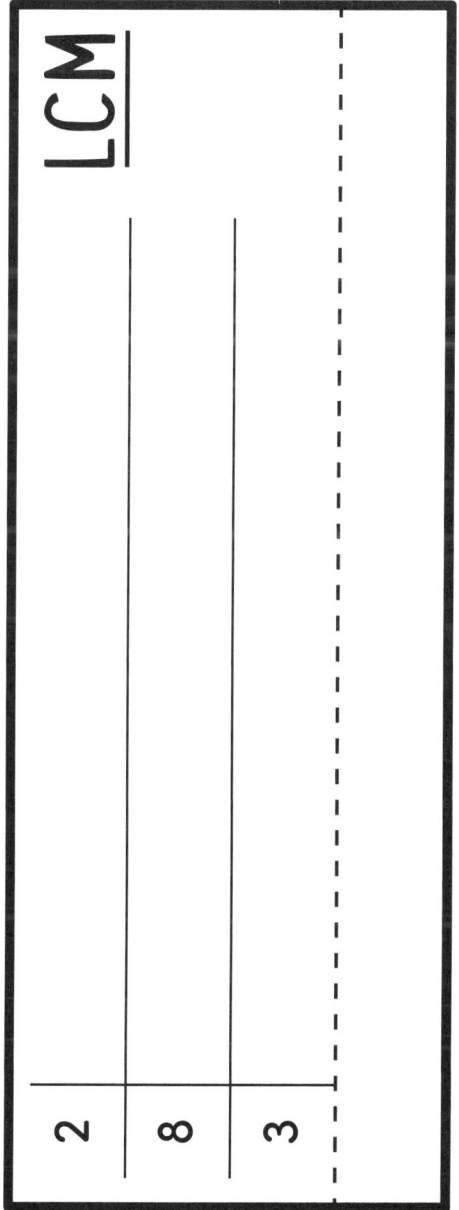

Multiplying Large Numbers

This lesson is designed to introduce one or more strategies at a time and can be taught during a period of days or weeks. If desired, each strategy may be placed on a separate page.

Introduction

Review basic multiplication facts. Have students stand in a line. Say a number to multiply by such as *twos* or *sevens*. Starting with the first student in line, students should say the products in order. For example, when multiplying by sevens, students should say *7, 14, 21, 28*, and so on. Then, challenge students to do the same thing with a factor that is a multiple of 10. For example, when multiplying by seventies, students should say *70, 140, 210, 280*, and so on.

Creating the Notebook Page

Guide students through the following steps to complete the right-hand page in their notebooks.

1. Add a Table of Contents entry for the Multiplying Large Numbers pages.

2. Cut out the title and glue it to the top of the page.

3. Cut out the *Standard Equation* piece. Cut on the solid lines at the top to create three flaps. Fold down the flaps over the numbers. Apply glue to the back of the title section and attach it to the page.

4. Solve each step of the problem with a different color. Lift the flap of each subsequent number to move to the next step. Record each step in the empty space to the right, writing each step in the matching color. Write notes and tips under the flap.

5. Cut out both of the remaining rectangles. Apply glue to the back of the title sections and attach them to the bottom of the page.

6. Work through each example step by step to complete the front of each flap. You may choose to use different colors to show separate steps of each method. As you work through each method, write notes and tips under the flap. For example, you may want to note that the Partial Products method splits up the large factor using expanded notation.

Reflect on Learning

To complete the left-hand page, have students convert their birthdays to three- or four-digit numbers. For example, October 8 would be 1,008. Then, students should multiply their birthday numbers by each factor 1 to 9.

Multiplying Large Numbers

Standard Equation

$$\begin{array}{r} 3{,}814 \\ \times \quad 2 \\ \hline \end{array}$$

Partial Products

3,814 × 2

× 2 =

× 2 =

× 2 =

× 2 = ________

Area Model

3,814 × 2

	3,000	800	10	4
2				

\+ ________

Multiplying Two-Digit Numbers

This lesson is designed to introduce one or more strategies at a time and can be taught during a period of days or weeks. If desired, each strategy may be placed on a separate page.

Introduction

Review multiplying large numbers by one digit. Have students solve several problems. Then, have students solve one of the same problems, but with the single-digit factor replaced by a multiple of 10. For example, if students previously solved *347 × 2*, have them solve *347 × 20*. Then, briefly discuss strategies they used to find the new product.

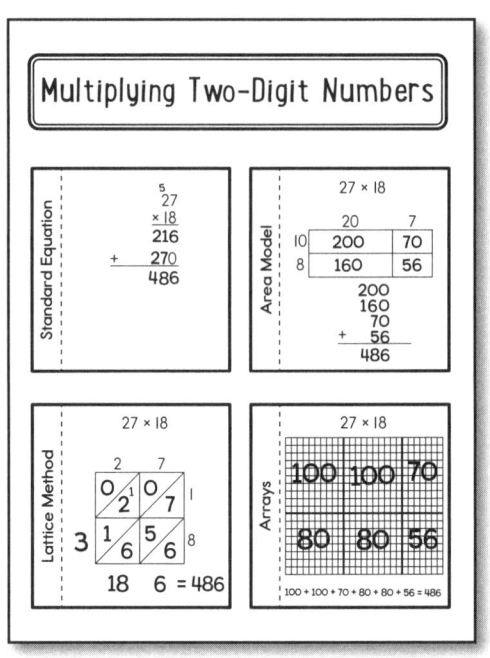

Creating the Notebook Page

Guide students through the following steps to complete the right-hand page in their notebooks.

1. Add a Table of Contents entry for the Multiplying Two-Digit Numbers pages.

2. Cut out the title and glue it to the top of the page.

3. Cut out each square. Apply glue to the back of the title section and attach each square to the page.

4. Work through each example step by step to complete the front of each flap. You may choose to use different colors to show separate steps of each method. As you work through each method, write notes and tips under the flap. For example, you may want to label the tens and ones sections in the lattice method or make a note that there is always a zero in the second line of the standard algorithm because you're always multiplying by a multiple of 10 in that step.

Reflect on Learning

To complete the left-hand page, have students solve several two-digit by two-digit multiplication problems using a method or methods of their choosing.

Multiplying Two-Digit Numbers

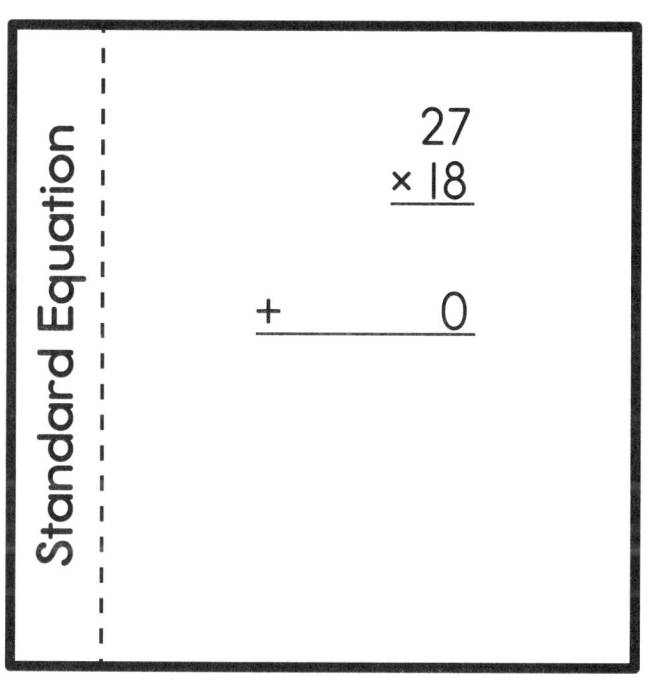

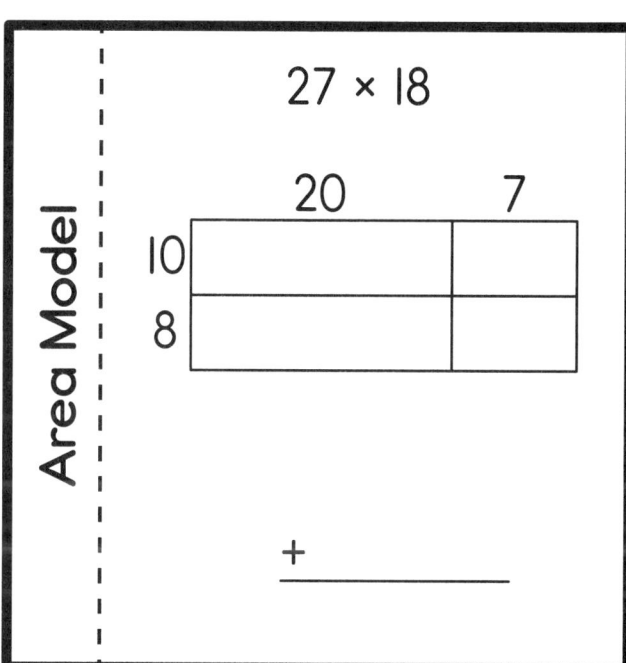

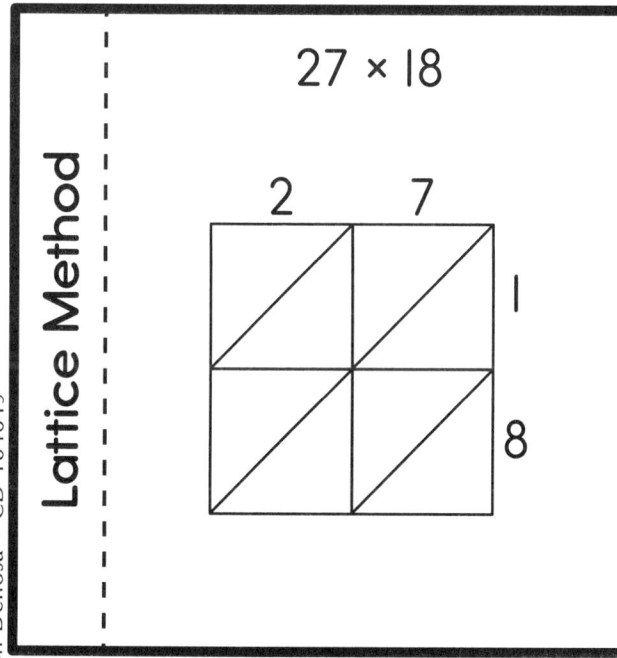

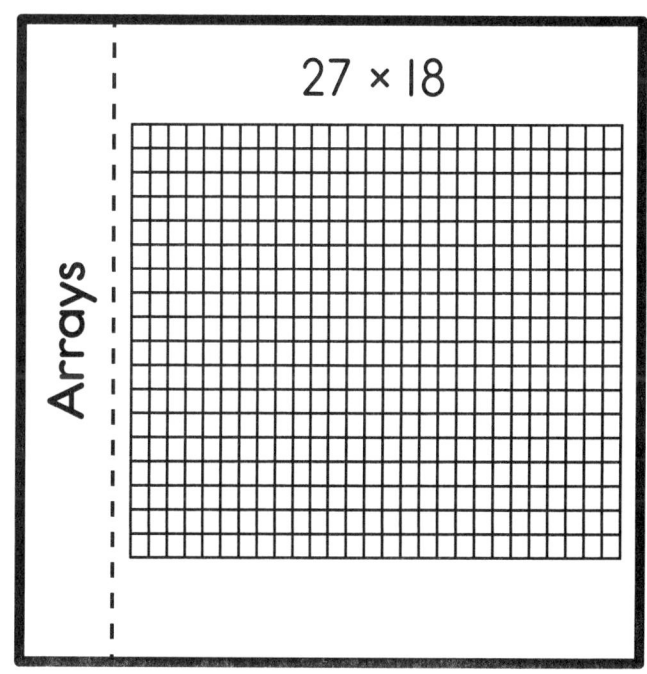

Dividing Large Numbers

This lesson is designed to introduce one or more strategies at a time and can be taught during a period of days or weeks. If desired, each strategy may be placed on a separate page.

Introduction

Review simple division facts. Have students solve several problems with partners. Then, have students solve one of the same problems, but with the dividend replaced by a multiple of 10. For example, if students previously solved *24 ÷ 4*, have them solve *240 ÷ 4*. Then, briefly discuss strategies they used to find the new quotient.

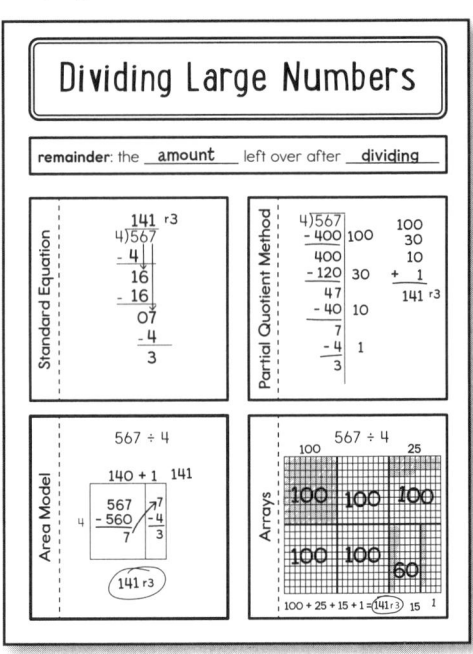

Creating the Notebook Page

Guide students through the following steps to complete the right-hand page in their notebooks.

1. Add a Table of Contents entry for the Dividing Large Numbers pages.

2. Cut out the title and glue it to the top of the page.

3. Cut out the *remainder* piece. Glue it below the title.

4. Complete the definition for *remainder* (the **amount** left over after **dividing**).

5. Cut out each square. Apply glue to the back of the title section and attach each square to the page.

6. Work through each example step by step to complete the front of each flap. You may choose to use different colors to show separate steps of each method. As you work through each method, write notes and tips under the flap. For example, you may want to add a note about how to handle a zero in a dividend in the standard equation or a hint about starting with multiples of 10 in the Partial Quotient Method.

Reflect on Learning

To complete the left-hand page, have students solve several division problems with a single-digit divisor and a two- to four-digit dividend using a method or methods of their choosing.

Dividing Large Numbers

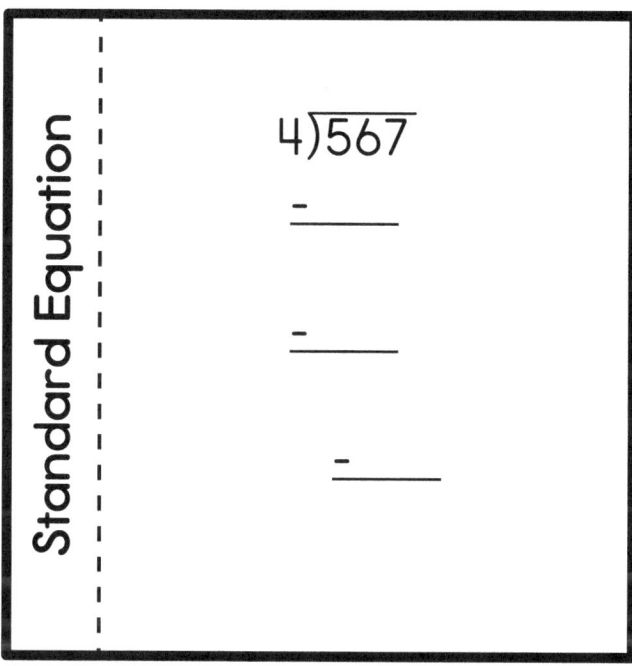

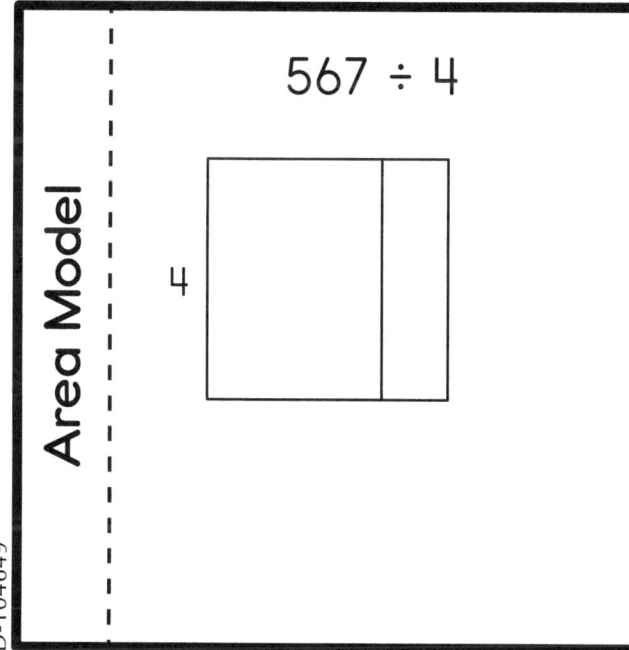

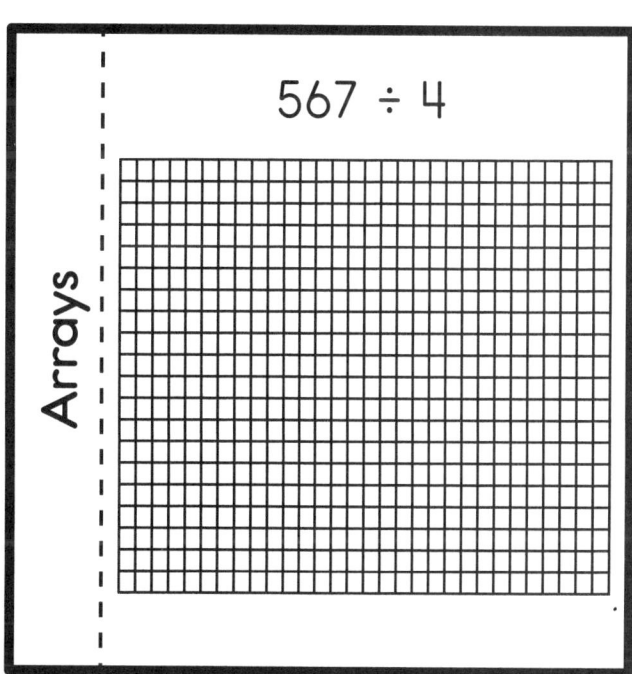

remainder: the _____ left over after _____

Equivalent Fractions

Introduction

Review fractions with students. Have them hold up 10 fingers. Say fractions such as $\frac{9}{10}$, $\frac{5}{10}$, or $\frac{2}{10}$, and have students hold up fingers to show the correct fraction. For example, for $\frac{2}{10}$, students should hold up 2 out of 10 fingers.

Creating the Notebook Page

Guide students through the following steps to complete the right-hand page in their notebooks.

1. Add a Table of Contents entry for the Equivalent Fractions pages.

2. Cut out the title and glue it to the top of the page.

3. Complete the definition of *equivalent fractions* (two or more fractions that are **equal**).

4. Cut out each fraction bar. Complete the fractions to label each flap. You may choose to color each fraction bar a different color. Then, cut on the solid lines to create a separate flap for each piece of each fraction bar.

5. Apply glue to the back of the flap at the top of each fraction bar. Glue each bar down, overlapping the fraction bars slightly so that the top flaps disappear. It may be helpful to start gluing at the bottom instead of the top. You may choose to place the fraction bars in numeric order, or group the halves, fourths, and eighths, and the thirds and sixths.

6. Use the flaps to find equivalent fractions, calling attention to the amount of space the flaps take up. Write the equivalent fractions below the fraction bars.

7. Cut out the four-flap piece. Cut on the solid lines to create four flaps. Fold on the dashed line so that the gray glue section is on the back of the flap book. Apply glue to the gray glue section and attach it to the right side of the page.

8. Use the fraction bars to find equivalent fractions. Write the fractions under each flap.

Reflect on Learning

To complete the left-hand page, challenge students to make lists of fractions equivalent to $\frac{1}{5}$, $\frac{1}{6}$, $\frac{2}{3}$, and $\frac{3}{4}$. Then, at the bottom of the page, have students write a rule in their own words for finding equivalent fractions.

Equivalent Fractions
two or more fractions that are _____

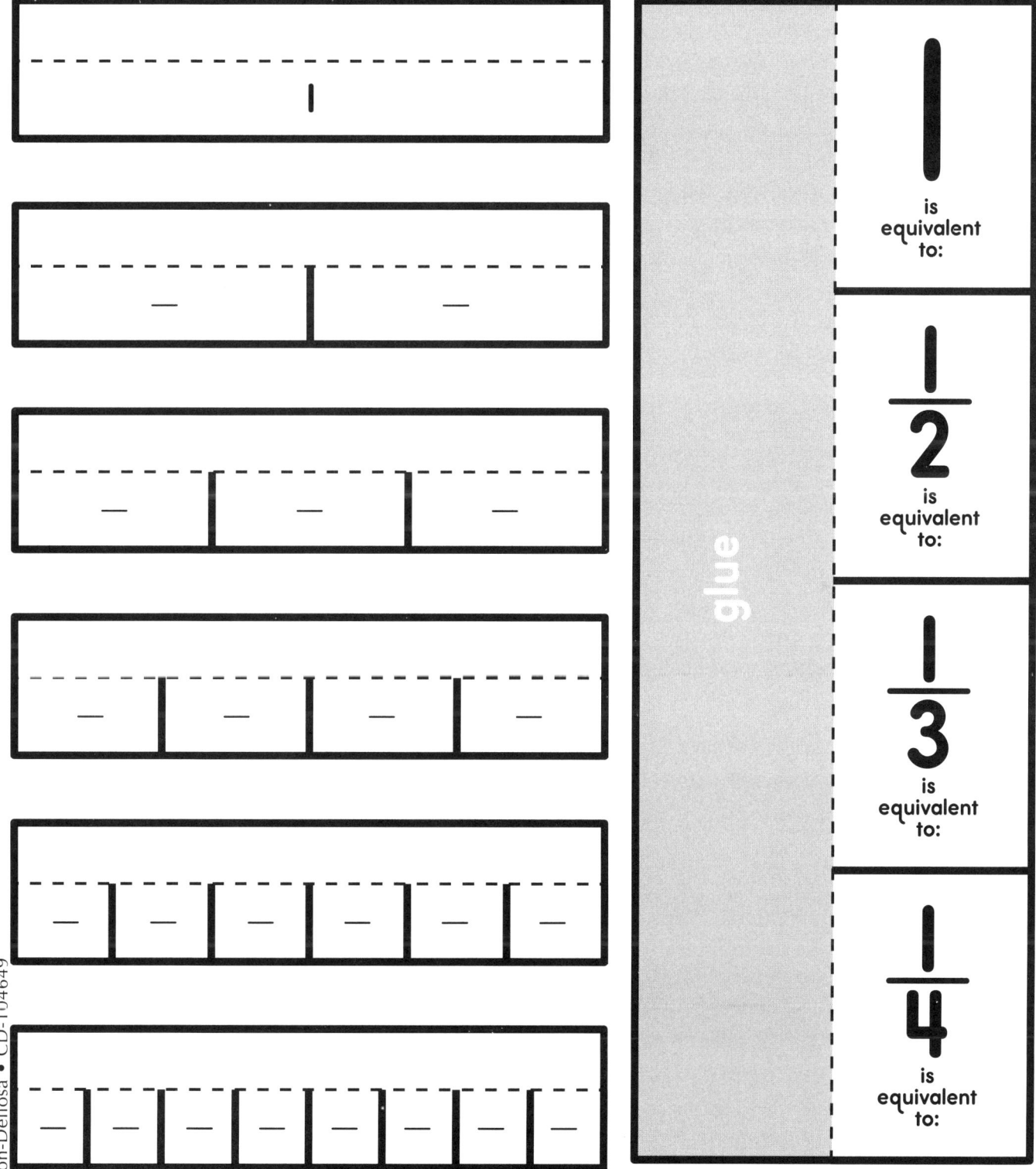

Adding and Subtracting Mixed Numbers

Introduction

Draw a circle and a square on the board. Divide each shape in half and shade in $\frac{1}{2}$. Discuss why you can't add those two fractions together. (They don't refer to parts of the same whole.) Then, draw two squares. Divide one into thirds and shade in $\frac{1}{3}$. Divide the other into eighths and shade in $\frac{1}{8}$. Discuss why you can't add those two fractions together. (They are from the same whole, but the pieces you are adding aren't the same size.)

Creating the Notebook Page

Guide students through the following steps to complete the right-hand page in their notebooks.

1. Add a Table of Contents entry for the Adding and Subtracting Mixed Numbers pages.

2. Cut out the title and glue it to the top of the page.

3. Cut out the *Strategies* flap book. Fold along the dashed lines to create two flaps. Apply glue to the back of the center section and attach it to the page below the title.

4. Cut out the rectangles with addition and subtraction problems. Apply glue to the back of each piece. Place the addition problem under the *Rename* strategy flap. Place the subtraction problem under the *Add or subtract* strategy flap.

5. Complete each example problem using the strategy presented on the flap. ($\frac{13}{4} + \frac{19}{4} = \frac{32}{4} = 8$) ($5\frac{2}{7} - 2\frac{4}{7} = 4\frac{9}{7} - 2\frac{4}{7} = 2\frac{5}{7}$)

6. Cut out the *Add or subtract* flap book. Cut on the solid lines to create six flaps. Apply glue to the back of the directions section and attach it to the bottom of the page.

7. Solve each problem using either strategy. Write the answer under each flap.

Reflect on Learning

To complete the left-hand page, have students record the problem $8\frac{1}{4} - 5\frac{3}{4}$. Students should draw a picture to show how you can "borrow" from the whole to make the fraction large enough to subtract from.

Answer Key
Clockwise from the top left: $7\frac{1}{3}$; 6; 11; $2\frac{5}{8}$; $10\frac{3}{4}$; $10\frac{2}{5}$

Adding and Subtracting Mixed Numbers

Strategies

Rename each mixed number as an improper fraction. Then, add or subtract. Simplify.

Add or subtract the fractions. Rename when needed. Then, add or subtract the whole numbers. Simplify.

$3\frac{1}{4} + 4\frac{3}{4} = \frac{}{4} + \frac{}{4} = \frac{}{4} =$

$5\frac{2}{7} - 2\frac{4}{7}$

$9\frac{2}{3} - 2\frac{1}{3}$

$5\frac{1}{4} + \frac{3}{4}$

$8\frac{4}{5} + 1\frac{3}{5}$

Add or subtract.

$6\frac{1}{2} + 4\frac{1}{2}$

$3\frac{3}{8} + 7\frac{3}{8}$

$4\frac{2}{8} - 1\frac{5}{8}$

Multiplying Fractions and Whole Numbers

Each student will need a brass paper fastener to complete this page.

Introduction

Review the parts of a fraction by playing a simple version of Simon Says. When Simon Says *numerator*, students should stand with their arms in the air to represent the upper part of the fraction. When Simon Says *denominator*, students should squat to represent the lower part of a fraction.

Creating the Notebook Page

Guide students through the following steps to complete the right-hand page in their notebooks.

1. Add a Table of Contents entry for the Multiplying Fractions and Whole Numbers pages.

2. Cut out the title and glue it to the top of the page.

3. Cut out the arrow piece. Starting with the arrow end on top, accordion fold on the dashed lines. Apply glue to the back of the last section. Attach it to the top left of the page.

4. Unfold the accordion. Shade the triangle a different color so that it stands out from the pieces behind it. Choose a fraction and a whole number to multiply. Write the multiplication sentence in the blank section on the far left. Then, use that problem to write an example below each of the three steps.

5. Cut out the *Hint!* mini file folder. Fold it in half along the dashed line. Apply glue to the back of the folder. Attach it to the right of the accordion arrow.

6. On the front of the folder, write a description of the hint (for example, *How to Change a Whole Number into a Fraction*). Open the folder. Write an example below the hint.

7. Cut out the circles and place the smaller circle on top. Push a brass paper fastener through the center dots of the circles to attach them. It may be helpful to create the hole in each piece separately first. Apply glue to the back of the large circle. Attach it to the bottom of the page with $\frac{1}{3}$ and $\frac{3}{8}$ at the top. Do not press the brass fastener through the page.

8. Spin the smaller circle around to create a variety of multiplication sentences. Include sentences that are whole numbers multiplied by fractions and fractions multiplied by whole numbers. Solve. Write the problems and answers around the circle.

Reflect on Learning

To complete the left-hand page, challenge students to draw a picture that shows how multiplying fractions and whole numbers works.

Multiplying Fractions and Whole Numbers

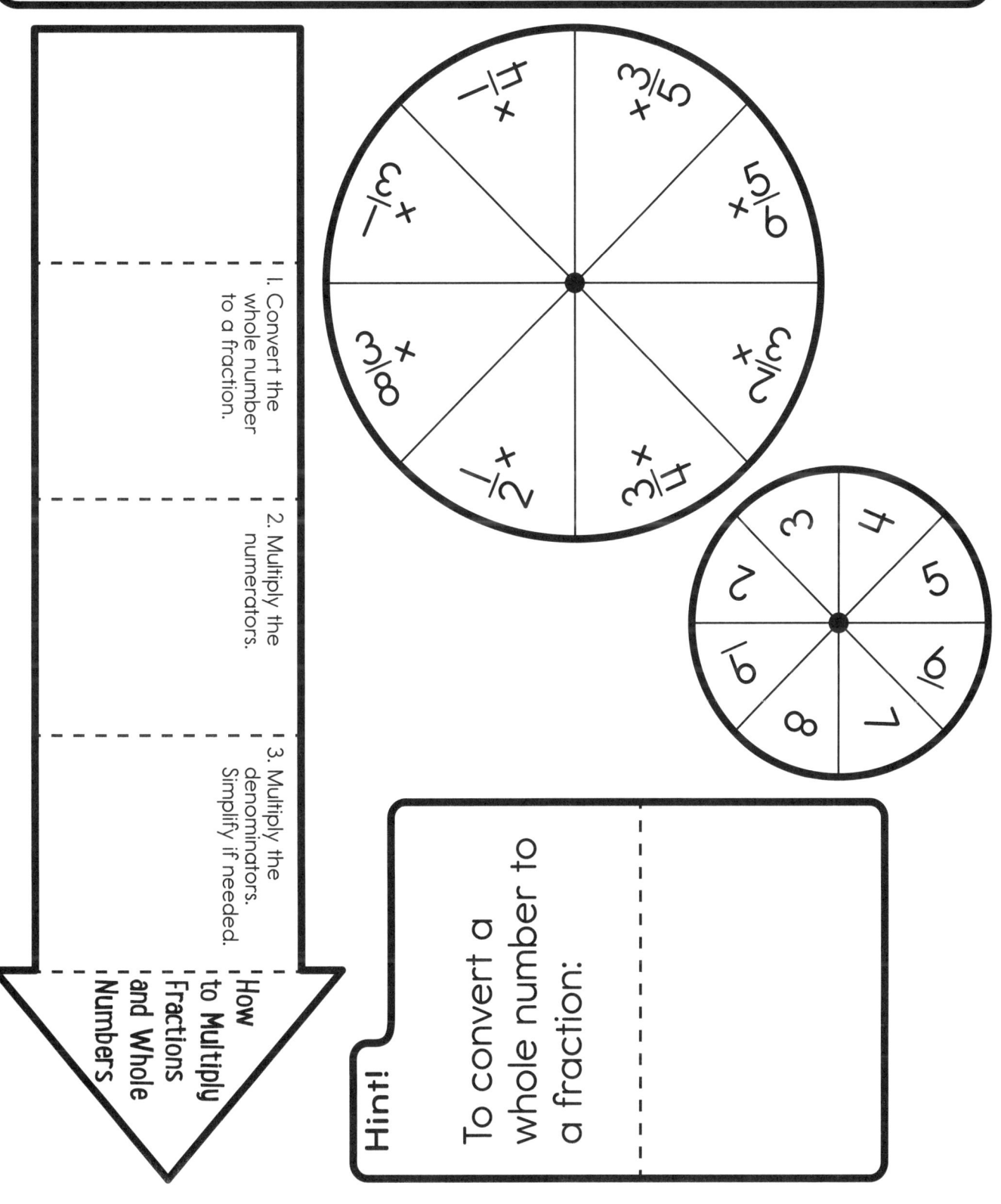

1. Convert the whole number to a fraction.
2. Multiply the numerators.
3. Multiply the denominators. Simplify if needed.

How to Multiply Fractions and Whole Numbers

Hint! To convert a whole number to a fraction:

Relating Fractions and Decimals

Introduction

Review fractions. Have students write the fractions for how many students in the class are wearing red, how many students have short hair, how many students are wearing short sleeves, etc.

Creating the Notebook Page

Guide students through the following steps to complete the right-hand page in their notebooks.

1. Add a Table of Contents entry for the Relating Fractions and Decimals pages.

2. Cut out the title and glue it to the top of the page.

3. Cut out the tenths and hundredths squares. Glue them side by side below the title.

4. Color in one-tenth. Then, complete the equation at the bottom by filling in the related fraction, decimal, and written forms ($\frac{1}{10}$ = **0.1** = **one-tenth**). Repeat with one hundredth on the other square ($\frac{1}{100}$ = **0.01** = **one-hundredth**).

5. Cut out the number line. Cut on the solid lines to create nine flaps. Apply glue to the back of the number line, 0, and 1. Attach it to the middle of the page.

6. On each flap, write the corresponding fraction. Under each flap, write the related decimal.

7. Cut out the *Convert* pieces. Cut on the solid lines to create five flaps. Apply glue to the back center of each piece. Attach each piece to the bottom of the page.

8. Write the answer to each problem under the flap.

Reflect on Learning

To complete the left-hand page, write a mixed number on the board. Ask students to describe how they would convert it to a decimal. Then, have students describe how they would add $\frac{26}{100} + \frac{5}{10}$. Students should use a number line or drawing to support their answers.

Answer Key
Convert to decimals: 0.3; 0.09; 0.8; 0.55; 0.70
Convert to fractions: $\frac{21}{100}$; $\frac{7}{10}$; $\frac{83}{100}$; $\frac{4}{10}$; $\frac{6}{100}$

Relating Fractions and Decimals

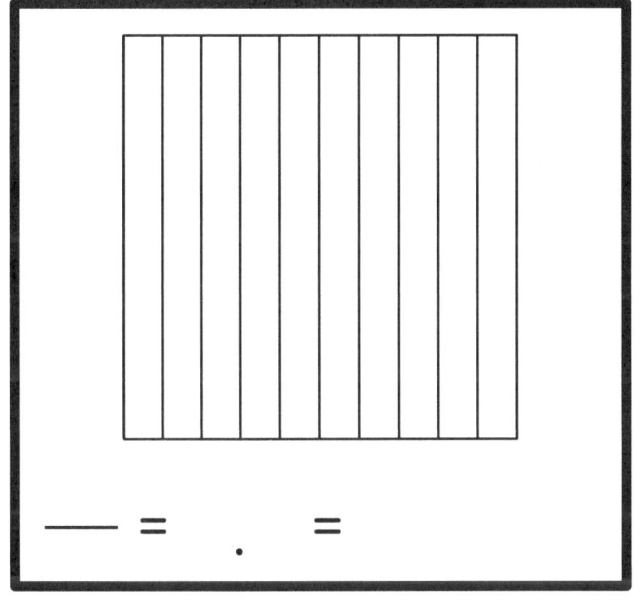

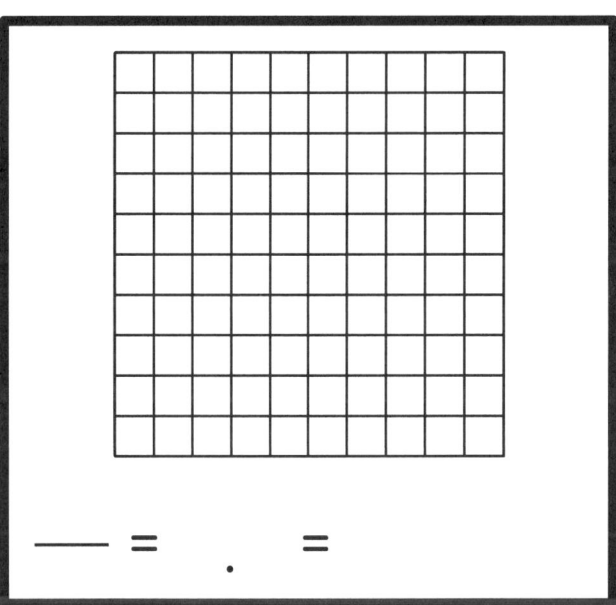

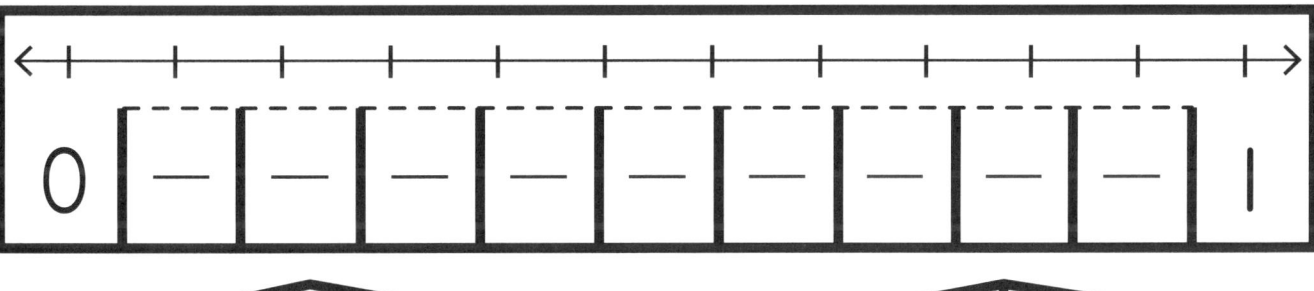

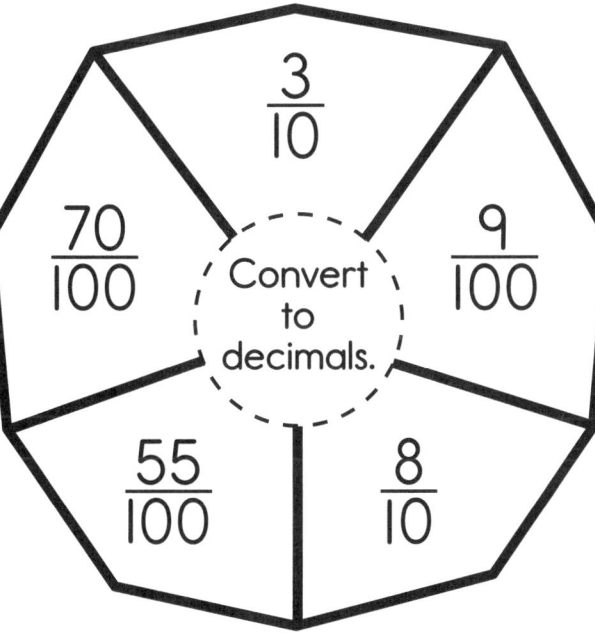

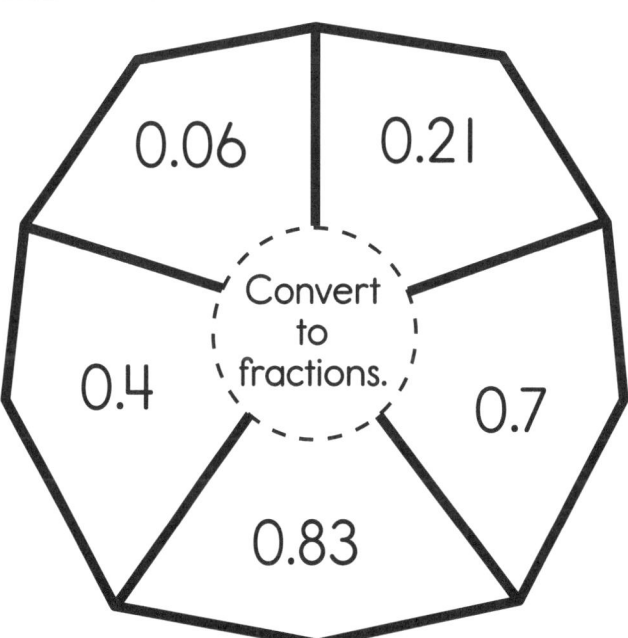

Comparing and Ordering Decimals

Introduction

Review comparing and ordering whole numbers. Write large numbers on index cards. Hand an index card to each student. Have pairs of students compare their numbers. Then, call on groups of three or more students to order their numbers from least to greatest or greatest to least.

Creating the Notebook Page

Guide students through the following steps to complete the right-hand page in their notebooks.

1. Add a Table of Contents entry for the Comparing and Ordering Decimals pages.

2. Cut out the title and glue it to the top of the page.

3. Cut out the *To compare decimals* piece and glue it to the top left of the page.

4. Complete the steps by filling in the blanks. (1. Align the numbers on the **decimal**. 2. Fill in empty place values with **zeros**. 3. Start with the **greatest** place value. 4. Move **right** until you find a **different** digit. 5. Then, compare using those **digits**.)

5. Cut out the piece with the equal sign. Fold the bottom and top flaps in over the equal sign. Apply glue to the back of the middle section. Attach it to the center of the bottom half of the page so that the flaps open up and down.

6. Flip the top flap down and draw a less than symbol (<) on it. Flip the bottom flap up and draw a greater than symbol (>) on it.

7. Cut out the pocket. Fold it in half. Apply glue to the back of the tabs. Fold the tabs around the back to create a pocket. Apply glue to the back of the pocket. Attach it to the page beside the *To compare decimals* piece.

8. Cut out the number cards. Place one card on each side of the symbols piece. Unfold the flaps to create a true number comparison. Or, choose three or more cards to place in order from least to greatest or greatest to least. For more practice, write additional decimals on the backs of the cards. Store the cards in the pocket.

Reflect on Learning

To complete the left-hand page, have students compare and contrast the process of comparing and ordering whole numbers, fractions, and decimals. Students should include examples to support their explanations.

Comparing and Ordering Decimals

3.4	3.44	34.8
4.68	8.68	41.7

=

To compare decimals:

1. Align the numbers on the _____.
2. Fill in empty place values with _____.
   3.49
   3.8 ↑
3. Start with the _____ place value.
4. Move _____ until you find a _____ digit.
5. Then, compare using those _____.

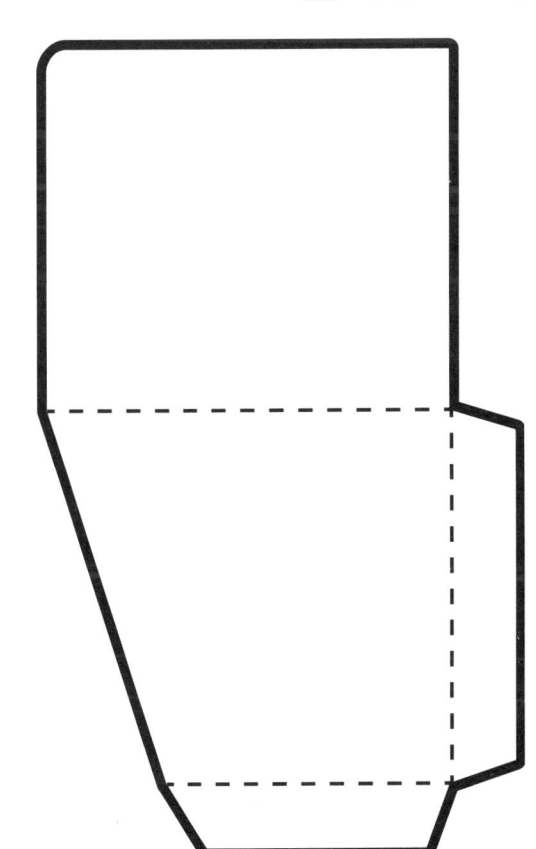

Adding and Subtracting Decimals

Introduction

Write .9, 0.9, and 0.90 on the board. Discuss the role of the zero in each number and how it affects the number. Then, add 0.09 to the list. Discuss how adding the zero before the 9 affects its value. As a class, generate a list of where a zero can be added to a decimal without changing its value.

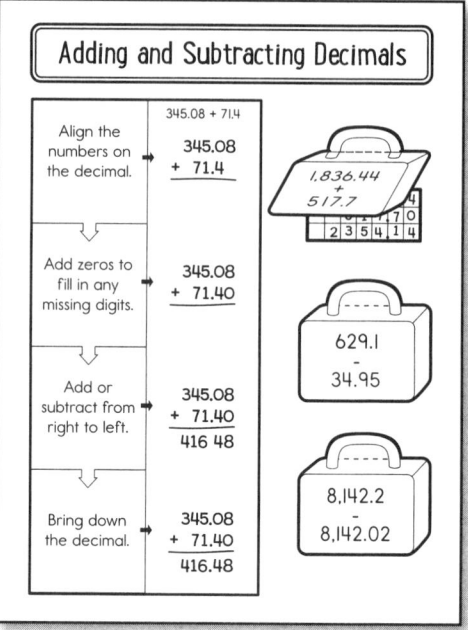

Creating the Notebook Page

Guide students through the following steps to complete the right-hand page in their notebooks.

1. Add a Table of Contents entry for the Adding and Subtracting Decimals pages.

2. Cut out the title and glue it to the top of the page.

3. Cut out the tall step-by-step piece and glue it to the left side of the page.

4. Read through the steps. Using the addition problem at the top of the right column, complete an example for each step in the process.

5. Cut out the locks. Fold each lock on the dashed line. Apply glue to the back of the top of each lock. Attach each lock along the right side of the page.

6. Cut out the three pieces of graph paper. Apply glue to the back of each piece and glue one under each lock so that it is hidden under the lock.

7. Rewrite each problem on the graph paper. Solve.

Reflect on Learning

To complete the left-hand page, have students reflect on the purpose of adding zeros to decimals when adding and subtracting. They should address why it is necessary, where zeros can and cannot be added, and how adding and subtracting whole numbers compares to adding and subtracting decimals. They may choose to add examples and illustrations to support their ideas.

Answer Key
From top to bottom: 2,354.14; 594.15; 0.18

Adding and Subtracting Decimals

Align the numbers on the decimal. →	345.08 + 71.4
Add zeros to fill in any missing digits. →	
Add or subtract from right to left. →	
Bring down the decimal. →	

1,836.44
+
517.7

629.1
-
34.95

8,142.2
-
8,142.02

Adding and Subtracting Decimals

Is It Reasonable?

Introduction

Write a simple math fact on the board with an obviously wrong answer (for example, 1 + 1 = 3 or 2 × 5 = 20). Discuss with the class how they know the answers are incorrect and why it is easy to immediately know that those answers are wrong. Then, have students discuss in small groups why it isn't as easy to notice wrong answers with more complicated problems. Have each group come up with a reason why it is important to be able to find wrong answers quickly. Allow each group to share with the class.

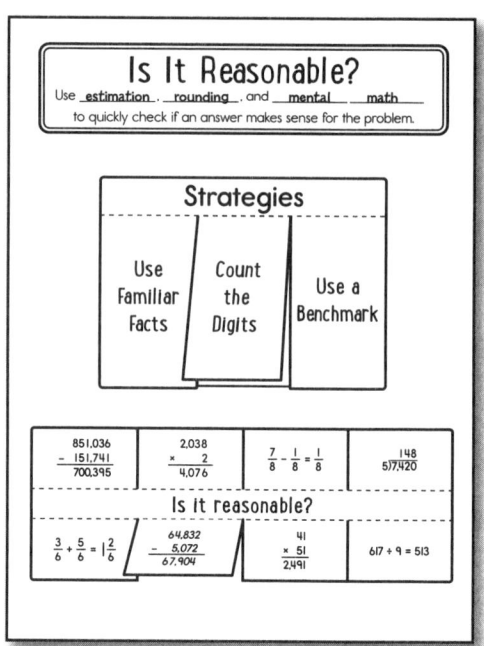

Creating the Notebook Page

Guide students through the following steps to complete the right-hand page in their notebooks.

1. Add a Table of Contents entry for the Is It Reasonable? pages.

2. Cut out the title and glue it to the top of the page.

3. Complete the sentence that explains the title. (Use **estimation**, **rounding**, and **mental math** to quickly check if an answer makes sense for the problem.)

4. Cut out the *Strategies* three-flap book and the matching example three-flap book. Cut on the solid lines to create three flaps on each book. Apply glue to the gray glue section and place the *Strategies* piece on top to created a stacked six-flap book. Apply glue to the back of the *Strategies* flap and attach it below the title.

5. Read through the example under each strategy. Then, complete the sample problem under the flap to support the explanation.

6. Cut out the *Is it reasonable?* flap book. Cut on the solid lines to create eight flaps. Apply glue to the back of the center section of the flap book. Attach it to the bottom of the page.

7. Check each problem using one of the three strategies. Under the flap, write *yes* or *no* to tell if the answer given is reasonable. Write a short explanation to support your answer.

Reflect on Learning

To complete the left-hand page, have students choose a strategy and explain it in their own words. Then, students should each write an example to support the explanation.

Answer Key
Top row: yes, yes, no, no; Bottom row: yes, no, yes, no

Is It Reasonable?

Use _____, _____, and _____ _____ to quickly check if an answer makes sense for the problem.

Strategies

- Use a Benchmark
- Count the Digits
- Use Familiar Facts

$\frac{3}{4} + \frac{3}{4} = \frac{6}{8}$

No! Because $\frac{3}{4}$ is greater than $\frac{1}{2}$. $\frac{1}{2} + \frac{1}{2} = 1$, so $\frac{3}{4} + \frac{3}{4}$ has to be greater than 1.

$37 \times 24 = 88$

No! Because $4 \times 2 = 8$, and 40×20 should have two zeros. The full answer should have three digits.

$6\overline{)3,648} = 501$

No! Because $36 \div 6 = 6$, so $3,600 \div 6 = 600$. The answer should be closer to 600.

Is it reasonable?

| 851,036 − 151,741 = 700,395 | 2,038 × 2 = 4,076 | $\frac{7}{8} - \frac{1}{8} = \frac{1}{8}$ | $5\overline{)7,420} = 148$ |
| $\frac{3}{6} + \frac{5}{6} = 1\frac{2}{6}$ | 64,832 − 5,072 = 67,904 | 41 × 51 = 2,491 | 617 ÷ 9 = 513 |

Patterns

Introduction

Draw several simple shape patterns on the board (for example, circle, rectangle, circle, rectangle and square, square, triangle, square, square, triangle). Have students draw the next three shapes for each pattern. Discuss how they knew what shapes to draw.

Creating the Notebook Page

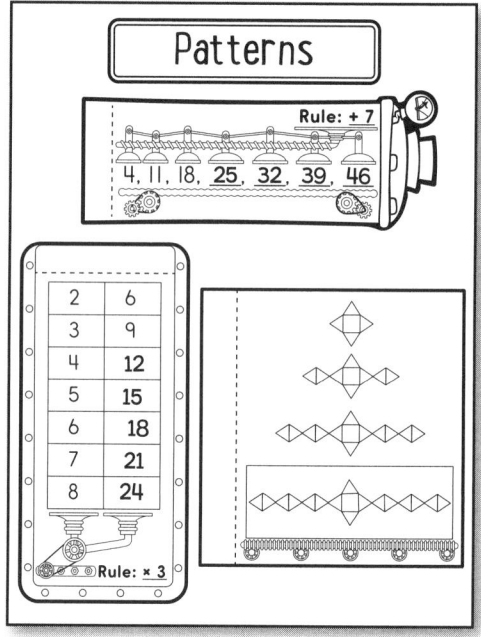

Guide students through the following steps to complete the right-hand page in their notebooks.

1. Add a Table of Contents entry for the Patterns pages.

2. Cut out the title and glue it to the top of the page.

3. Cut out the three remaining pieces. Apply glue to the back of the narrow section of each flap. Glue the row of numbers piece below the title. Glue the chart and shape pattern pieces side by side at the bottom of the page.

4. Use the given information on each piece to fill in the missing information. Discuss how patterns can come in many forms and how there are different ways of discovering each unique pattern.

5. Under each flap, record additional patterns you notice on the front of the flap. For example, describe how much the number of lines increases each time on the shape pattern or describe the pattern of even and odd numbers on the chart.

Reflect on Learning

To complete the left-hand page, have students create a number pattern and a shape pattern. They should write a rule for each and list any additional patterns they notice for each one.

Answer Key
+ 7: 25, 32, 39, 46; × 3: 12, 15, 18, 21, 24; The shape pattern should have a pair of triangles added to both the left and right sides.

Patterns

Rule: + 7

4, 11, 18, ___, ___, ___, ___

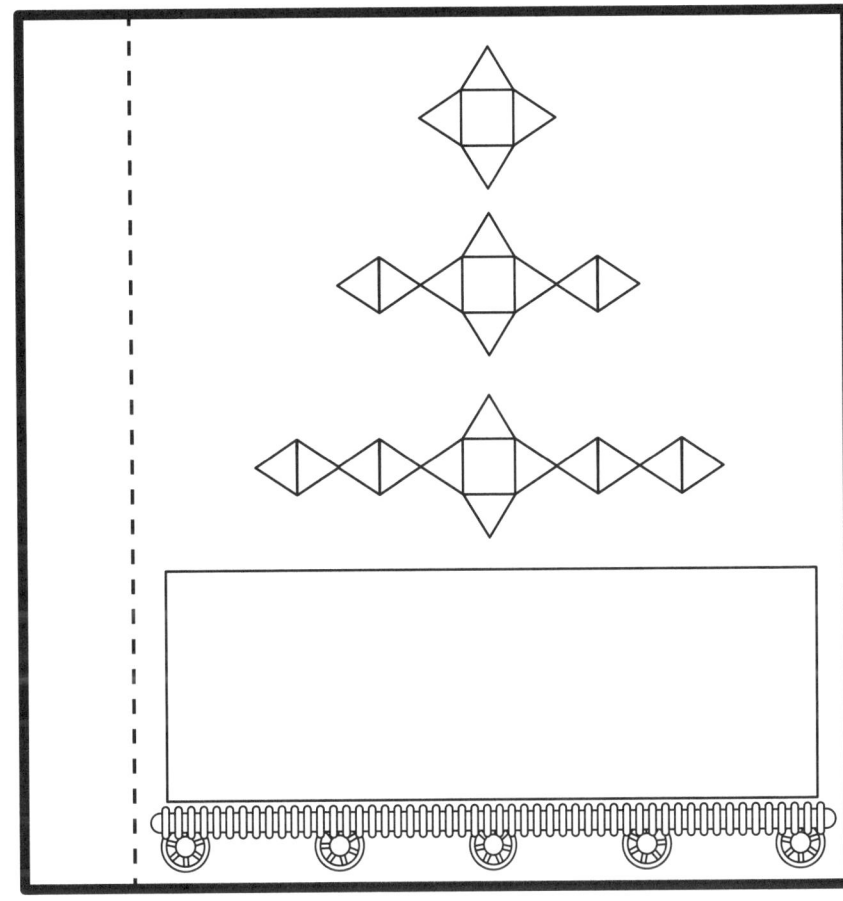

	2	3	4	5	6	7	8
	6	9					

Rule: × 3

Unknown Numbers

Introduction

Write several multiplication and division facts on the board with symbols such as a question mark or a box to replace one of the numbers in each fact (for example, 3 × ? = 36). Ask students to complete each fact. Then, challenge the class to describe how they knew the correct number for each placeholder.

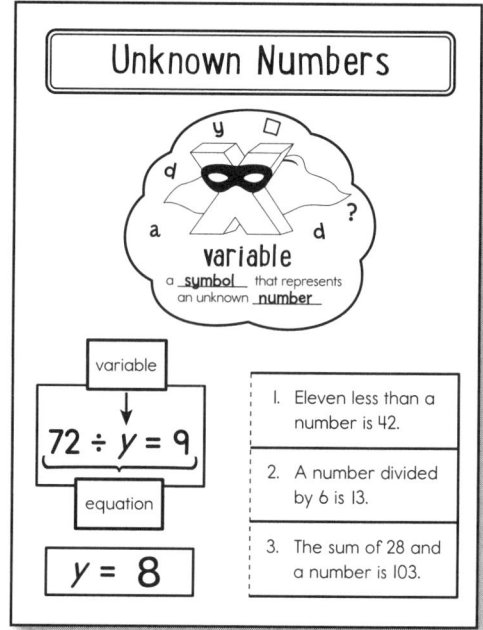

Creating the Notebook Page

Guide students through the following steps to complete the right-hand page in their notebooks.

1. Add a Table of Contents entry for the Unknown Numbers pages.

2. Cut out the title and glue it to the top of the page.

3. Cut out the cloud-shaped piece and glue it below the title.

4. Complete the definition of *variable* (a **symbol** that represents an unknown **number**). Discuss how variables can be any letter of the alphabet, or even shapes or other symbols. Fill in the space around the character with more examples of variables.

5. Cut out the equation and labels pieces. Glue the equation to the bottom left of the page, leaving space above and below. Glue the vocabulary words above the arrow and under the bracket to correctly label the parts of the equation. Then, complete the answer piece ($y = 8$). Glue it below the equation.

6. Cut out the word equations flap book. Cut on the solid lines to create three flaps. Fold the flaps on the dashed line to create the flap book. Apply glue to the gray glue section and attach it to the bottom-right side of the page.

7. Read the problem on each flap. Under the flap, write an equation with a variable that will help solve the problem. Then, solve.

Reflect on Learning

To complete the left-hand page, write several simple equations with variables, such as $x + 30 = 124$, on the board. Have students write a word problem to go along with each equation. Then, students should solve each problem.

Answer Key
1. $x - 11 = 42$; $x = 53$; 2. $x \div 6 = 13$; $x = 78$; 3. $28 + x = 103$; $x = 75$

Unknown Numbers

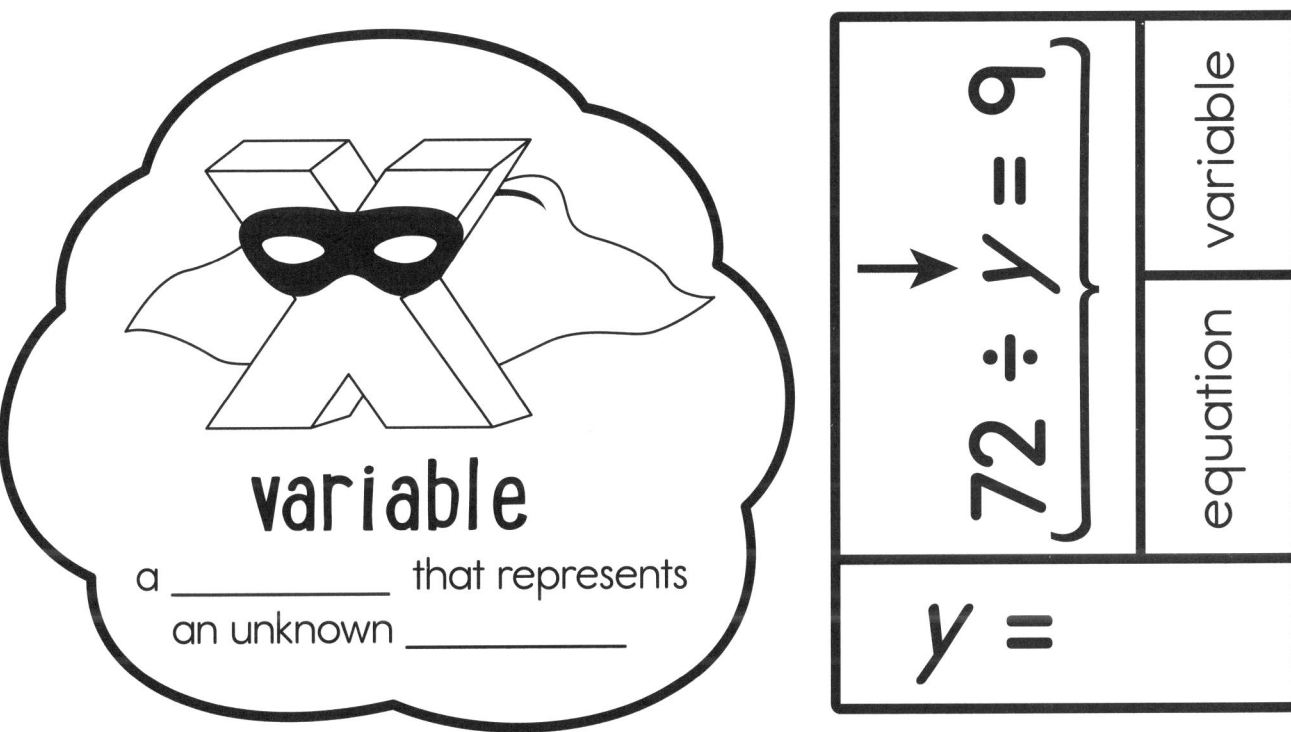

variable
a _____ that represents an unknown _____

$72 \div y = 9$ → variable / equation

$y =$

glue

1. Eleven less than a number is 42.

2. A number divided by 6 is 13.

3. The sum of 28 and a number is 103.

Converting Measurements

Introduction

Ask students to imagine a creature in their classroom that is 600 centimeters long. Have several students show how much space they think it would take up. Then, tell students there is a different creature that is 6 meters long. Have a few students show how much space they think this new creature would take up. Tell students that both creatures are the same length. Discuss how using different units can make measurements easier to understand and how converting between measurements can be helpful.

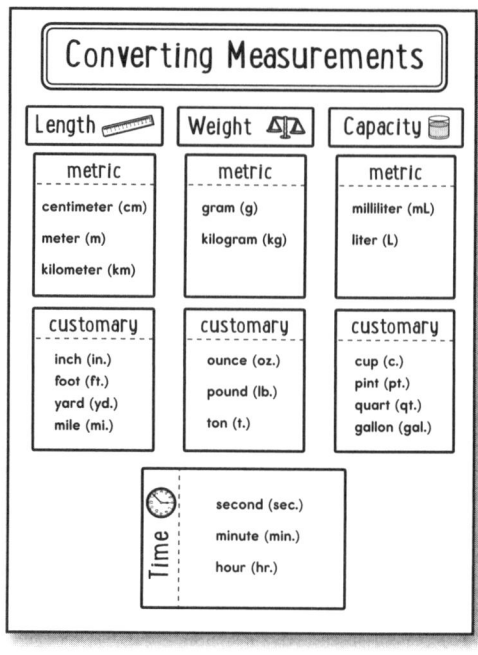

Creating the Notebook Page

Guide students through the following steps to complete the right-hand page in their notebooks.

1. Add a Table of Contents entry for the Converting Measurements pages.

2. Cut out the title and glue it to the top of the page.

3. Cut out the *Length*, *Weight*, and *Capacity* pieces. Glue them in a row below the title.

4. Cut out the metric and customary flaps. Apply glue to the back of each top section and attach it to the page below the correct label.

5. Cut out the *Time* flap. Apply glue to the back of the left side and attach it to the bottom of the page.

6. Under each flap, write common conversions (for example, 1 ft. = 12 in., or 1,000 g = 1 kg). Under the customary capacity flap, it may help to draw the big G (see below) to best show the relationships between the quantities.

Reflect on Learning

To complete the left-hand page, have students describe the differences they see between metric and customary measurements. Then, have students explain how to convert from one measurement to another within a system.

Converting Measurements

Time
- second (sec.)
- minute (min.)
- hour (hr.)

Length
Weight
Capacity

metric
- centimeter (cm)
- meter (m)
- kilometer (km)

metric
- gram (g)
- kilogram (kg)

metric
- milliliter (mL)
- liter (L)

customary
- inch (in.)
- foot (ft.)
- yard (yd.)
- mile (mi.)

customary
- ounce (oz.)
- pound (lb.)
- ton (t.)

customary
- cup (c.)
- pint (pt.)
- quart (qt.)
- gallon (gal.)

Elapsed Time

Introduction

Write your school's starting and ending times on the board, including *am* and *pm*. Ask students to estimate how much time they spend in school. Tell students that the amount of time that passes between two given times is called *elapsed time*, and there are several methods for finding the difference.

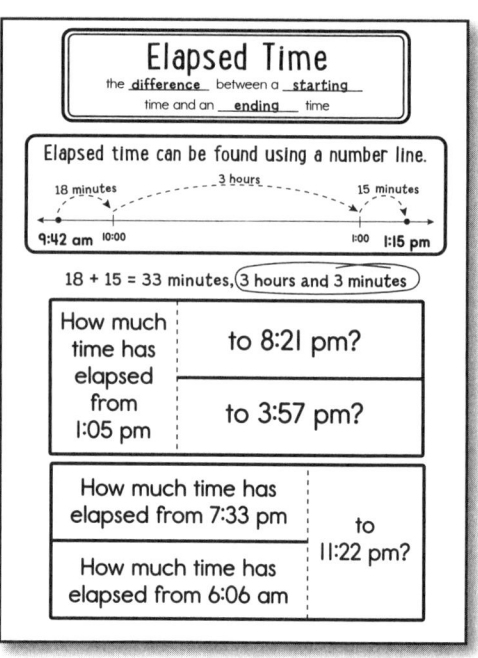

Creating the Notebook Page

Guide students through the following steps to complete the right-hand page in their notebooks.

1. Add a Table of Contents entry for the Elapsed Time pages.

2. Cut out the title and glue it to the top of the page.

3. Complete the definition for *elapsed time* (the **difference** between a **starting** time and an **ending** time).

4. Cut out the number line piece and glue it below the title.

5. Write amounts of time above each arrow to show how much time passed in that space. Discuss how you should always find three amounts on the number line: the time between the starting time and the next hour, the time between that hour and the whole hour immediately before the ending time, and the time between the whole hour and the ending time. Then, add those three amounts together to get the elapsed time. Write the elapsed time below the number line.

6. Cut out the two flap books. Cut on the solid lines to create two long flaps on each book. Apply glue to the back of the tall sections. Attach the flap books to the bottom of the page.

7. Under each flap, draw a number line to find the elapsed time.

Reflect on Learning

To complete the left-hand page, have students use the school start and end times to find the exact amount of time they spend at school each day.

Elapsed Time

the _____ between a _____ time and an _____ time

Elapsed time can be found using a number line.

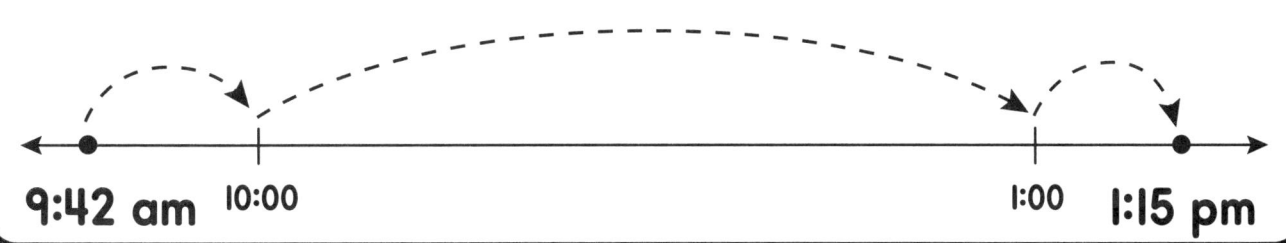

9:42 am   10:00   1:00   1:15 pm

| How much time has elapsed from 1:05 pm | to 8:21 pm? |
| | to 3:57 pm? |

| How much time has elapsed from 7:33 pm | to 11:22 pm? |
| How much time has elapsed from 6:06 am | |

Area and Perimeter

Introduction

Draw a rectangle on the board. Add a dog in the center if desired. Tell students that Mr. Katz wants to fence in an area for his dog and cover the entire space with sod. Have students discuss in small groups how he can measure for the fence and the sod. As a class, discuss whether he can use the same measurement for both.

Creating the Notebook Page

Guide students through the following steps to complete the right-hand page in their notebooks.

1. Add a Table of Contents entry for the Area and Perimeter pages.

2. Cut out the title and glue it to the top of the page.

3. Cut out the two single flaps. Apply glue to the gray glue area on the 5 by 7 rectangle piece and place the other flap on top of it. Then, apply glue to the back of the top section to attach the two-page flap book below the title.

4. Reinforce the difference between area and perimeter by using two different colors to trace the perimeter of the rectangle and shade in the area on the top flap. Use the same colors to outline and shade the 5 by 7 rectangle on the next flap.

5. Cut out the *area* and *perimeter* flap books. Cut on the solid lines to create three flaps on each flap book. Apply glue to the back of the title sections and attach each one to the page.

6. Write the definition, formula, and units under the corresponding flaps for both area and perimeter.

7. Return to the rectangles at the top of the page. Under the last flap, use the formulas to calculate the area and perimeter of the 5 by 7 rectangle.

Reflect on Learning

To complete the left-hand page, have students describe the difference between area and perimeter. Some students may choose to draw pictures, while other students may choose to write a paragraph or create a chart comparing and contrasting them. Then, tell students that Mr. Katz bought 100 feet of fencing for the pen. Have students find the biggest pen he can make for his dog and then find out how much sod he will need to buy for a pen of that size.

Area and Perimeter

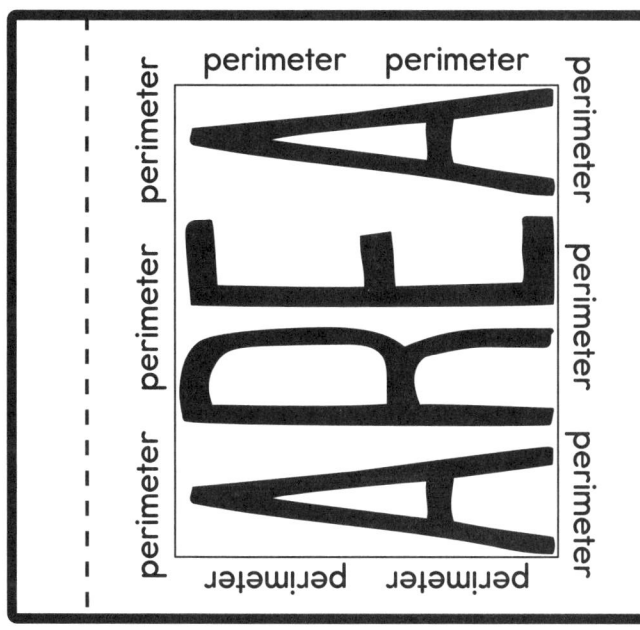
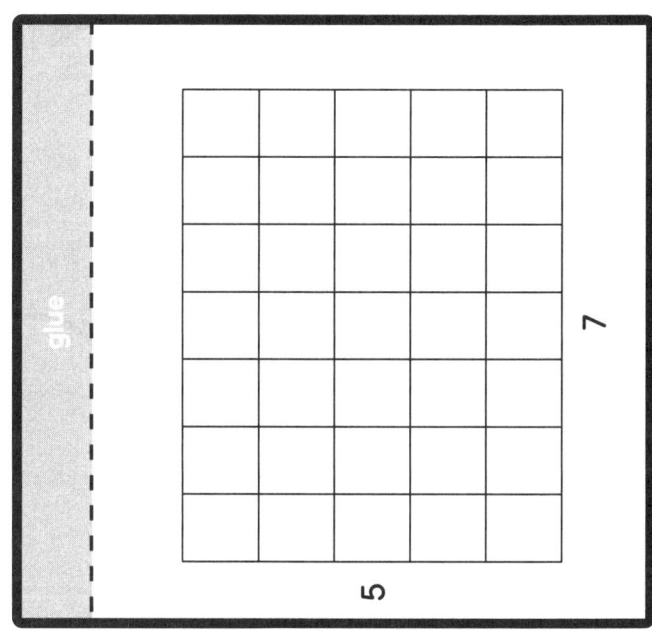
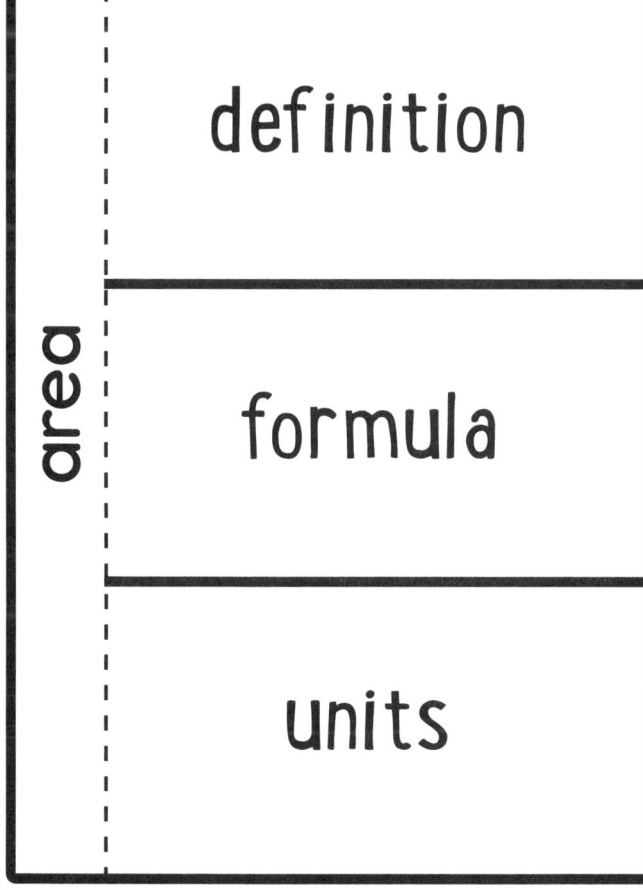
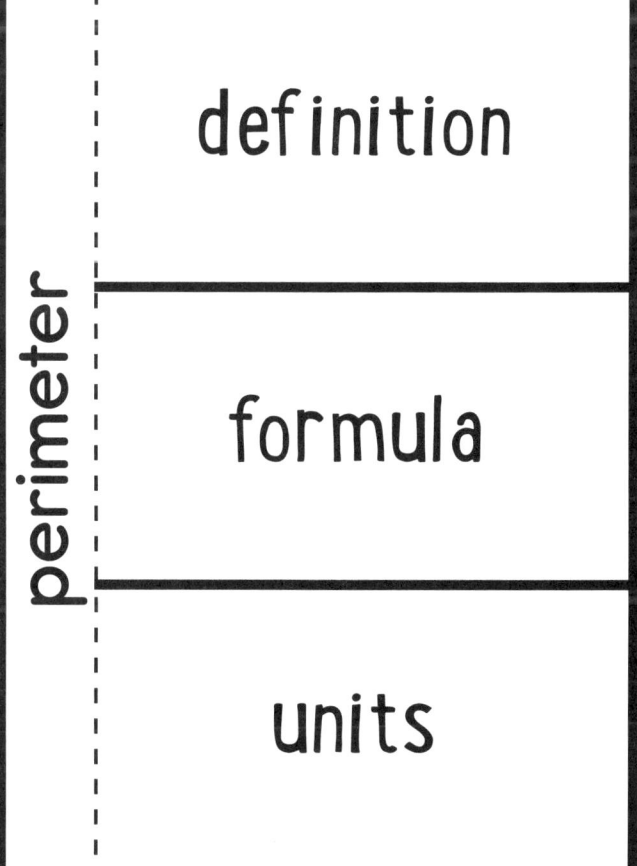

Line Plots

Introduction

Write a set of data on the board. Then, have small groups of students turn the data into different graphs such as bar graphs or stem-and-leaf plots. Allow each group to share their graph. As a class, discuss how the same data can look very different, depending on how it is presented. Discuss how some graphs are better for different things such as showing frequency or comparing categories of data.

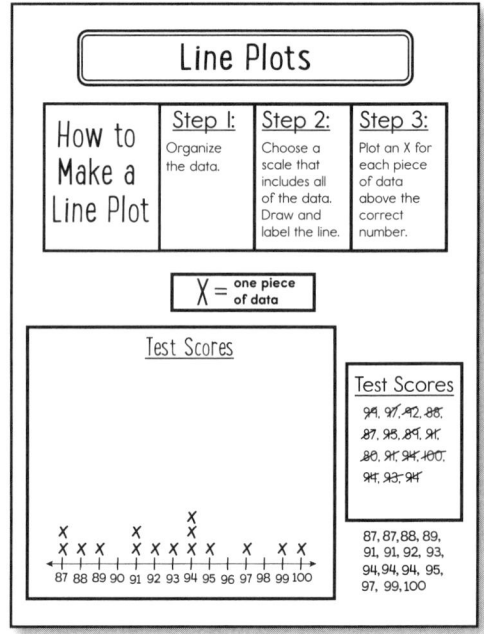

Creating the Notebook Page

Guide students through the following steps to complete the right-hand page in their notebooks.

1. Add a Table of Contents entry for the Line Plots pages.

2. Cut out the title and glue it to the top of the page.

3. Cut out the *Step 1, 2,* and *3* flaps and the *How to Make a Line Plot* piece. Fold each flap on the dashed line. Apply glue to the back of each small section. Start with *Step 3* by placing it on the right side of the page. Then, attach *Step 2* to the left so that the flap covers the blank section of the piece to the right. Repeat with each piece, gluing the entire title piece to the page last.

4. Under each of the *Step 1, 2,* and *3* flaps, write extra information or hints. For example, under the *Step 2* flap, you may choose to write that every number in the scale should be included, even if no data points fall on that number.

5. Cut out the *X =* piece. Glue it to the page below the steps.

6. Discuss how each X on a line plot stands for one piece of data. So, when drawing line plots, it is important that the Xs are the same size.

7. Cut out the blank line plot and *Test Scores* pieces. Glue the line plot to the bottom left of the page. Glue the test scores to the right of the line plot, leaving space below.

8. Using the test scores, follow the steps to complete the line plot.

Reflect on Learning

To complete the left-hand page, have students collect 10 crayons or colored pencils. Then, students should measure each one to the nearest quarter inch and record the data. Next, students should use the data to create a line plot. Finally, have students use the line plot to write three true statements about the data set.

Line Plots

X = one piece of data

Step 3: Plot an X for each piece of data above the correct number.

Step 2: Choose a scale that includes all of the data. Draw and label the line.

Step 1: Organize the data.

How to Make a Line Plot

Test Scores

Test Scores
99, 97, 92, 88, 87, 95, 89, 91, 80, 91, 94, 100, 94, 93, 94

Probability

Introduction

On opposite ends of the board, write *impossible* and *certain*. Have students add events under each category, such as *The sun will rise.* under *certain*, and *I will become 2 inches tall.* under *impossible*. Then, discuss how students would describe events that don't fall under either category, such as *I will eat pizza this week.*

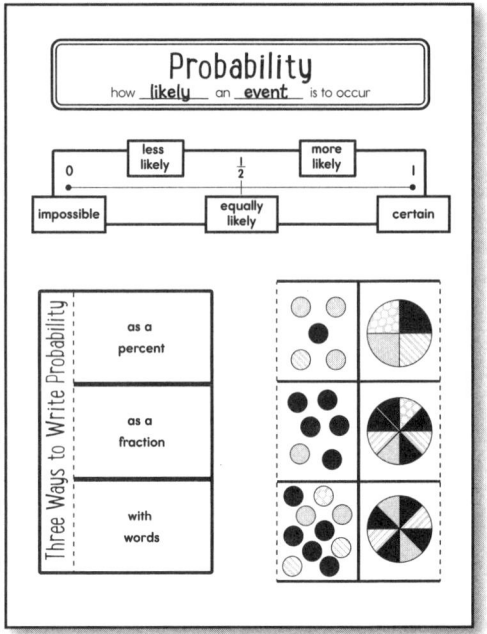

Creating the Notebook Page

Guide students through the following steps to complete the right-hand page in their notebooks.

1. Add a Table of Contents entry for the Probability pages.

2. Cut out the title and glue it to the top of the page.

3. Complete the definition of *probability* (how **likely** an **event** is to occur).

4. Cut out the number line and the five labels. Glue the number line to the top of the page.

5. Discuss each label and decide what part of the number line it best describes. Glue each term to the probability number line.

6. Next, cut out the *Three Ways to Write Probability* flap book. Cut on the solid lines to create three flaps. Apply glue to the back of the title section and attach it to the bottom left side of the page.

7. Under each flap, write an example such as *1 out of 2*, $\frac{1}{2}$, and *50%*. When discussing percentages, it may be helpful to refer to weather forecasts.

8. Cut out the shutter fold piece with the spinners and marble art. Cut on the solid lines to create six flaps. Then, place the piece with the art facedown and fold the flaps toward the center. Apply glue to the gray glue section and attach it to the bottom right of the page.

9. Write the probability of spinning a black section or drawing a black marble under each flap. If desired, you may also write the probabilities of spinning or drawing gray, stripes, or dots. You may choose to reduce fractions when possible.

Reflect on Learning

To complete the left-hand page, have students write their first names. Then, have students pretend the letters of their names were jumbled in a bag. Have them identify the probability of drawing a vowel, a consonant, a capital letter, a lowercase letter, a letter, and a number.

Probability
how _____ an _____ is to occur

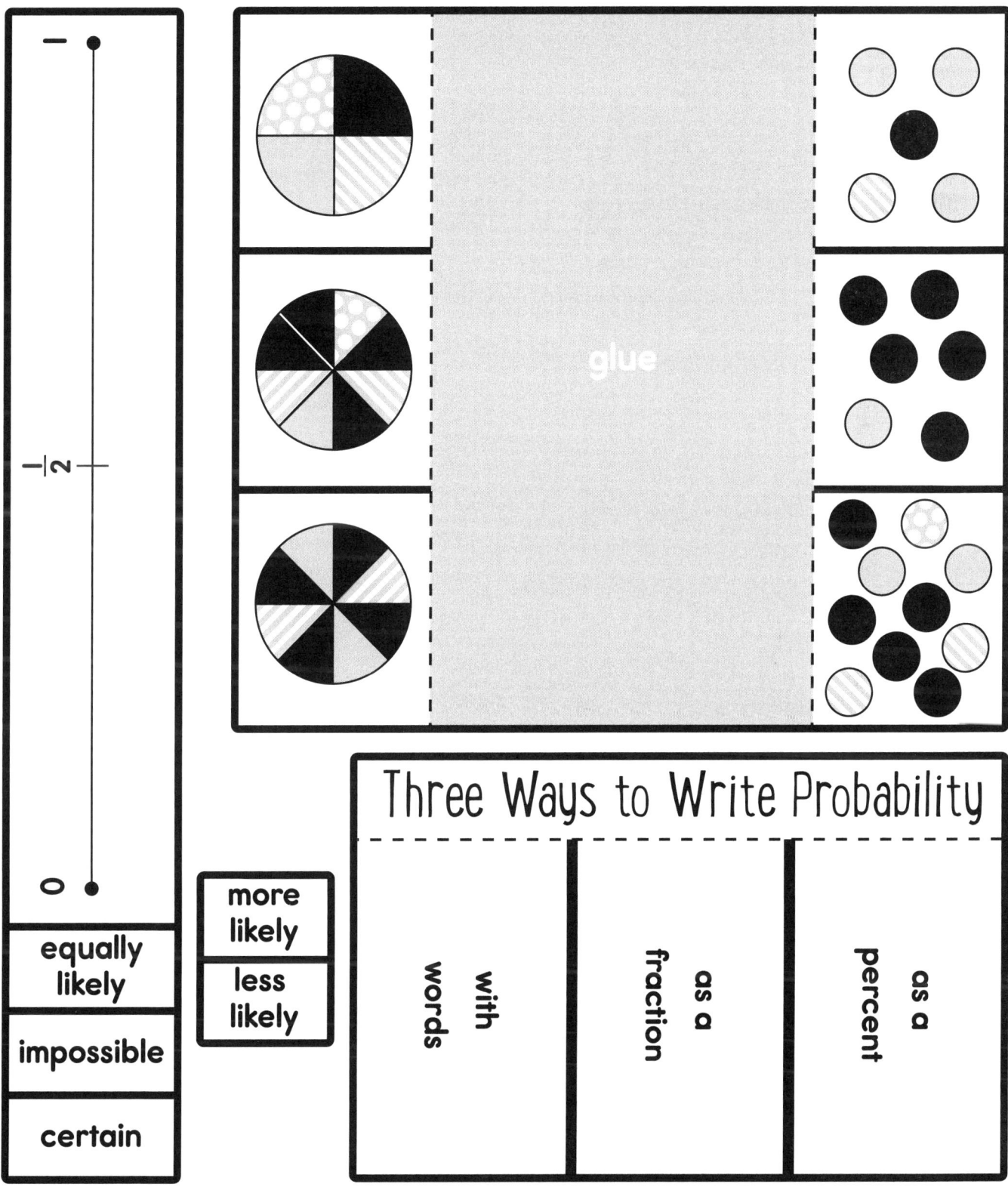

Three Ways to Write Probability
- with words
- as a fraction
- as a percent

- equally likely
- impossible
- certain
- more likely
- less likely

Points, Lines, and Rays

Introduction

Have students work in pairs. Challenge each pair to make fists with their hands and then work together to create different polygons with their forearms. As a class, discuss if a shape can be made by one person, and why it is or isn't possible. Explain that in geometry, there are names for the building blocks of polygons such as *points* and *lines*.

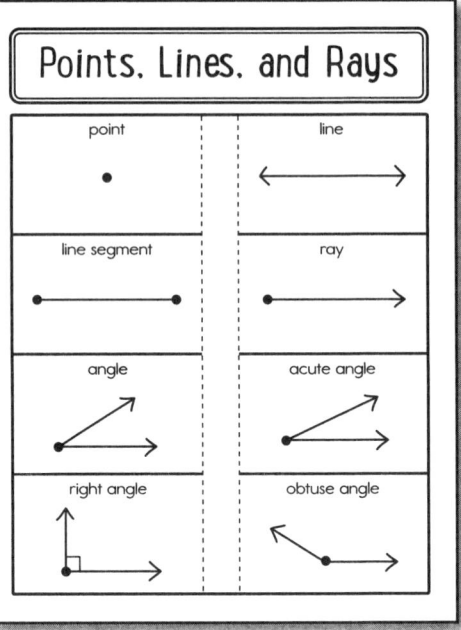

Creating the Notebook Page

Guide students through the following steps to complete the right-hand page in their notebooks.

1. Add a Table of Contents entry for the Points, Lines, and Rays pages.

2. Cut out the title and glue it to the top of the page.

3. Cut out the flap book. Cut on the solid lines to create eight flaps. If desired, cut off the bottom half to create a separate flap book for angles. Apply glue to the back of the center section and attach it to the page.

4. Discuss each geometry term. On each flap, draw an example of the term.

5. Under each flap, write a short definition for each geometry term.

Reflect on Learning

To complete the left-hand page, have students draw a chart with eight rows. Students should label each row with a geometry term from the opposite page. Then, they should identify real-world examples of each term and record each example in the chart.

Points, Lines, and Rays

point	line
line segment	ray
angle	acute angle
right angle	obtuse angle

Parallel and Perpendicular Lines

Introduction

Review lines, line segments, and the three main types of angles (acute, right, and obtuse). Challenge students to use two pencils to illustrate each geometry term.

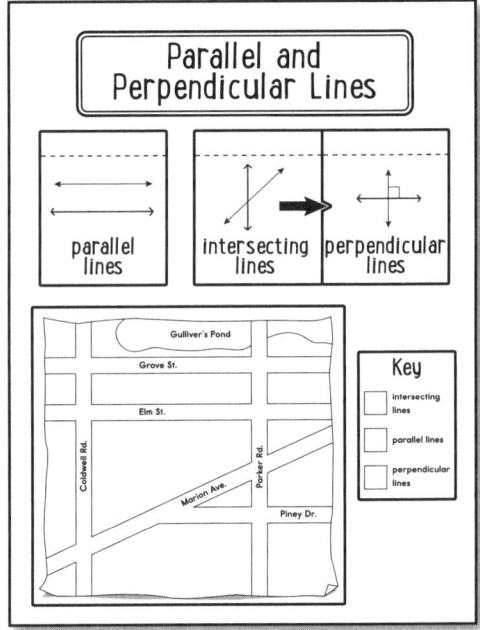

Creating the Notebook Page

Guide students through the following steps to complete the right-hand page in their notebooks.

1. Add a Table of Contents entry for the Parallel and Perpendicular Lines pages.

2. Cut out the title and glue it to the top of the page.

3. Cut out each rectangular flap. Take care to cut out the tip of the arrow on the *intersecting lines* piece. Apply glue to the back of the narrow section of each flap. Attach the flaps in a row below the title. Glue the *intersecting lines* and *perpendicular lines* pieces so that their sides touch.

4. Draw a line on each piece to complete the examples. Under each flap, write a definition in your own words. Discuss how perpendicular lines are a special type of intersecting lines.

5. Cut out the map and key. Glue them to the bottom of the page.

6. Use three different colors to fill the squares on the key. Then, using the correct colors, identify the parallel, intersecting, and perpendicular lines on the map. Some roads may be colored more than one color.

Reflect on Learning

To complete the left-hand page, have students write the uppercase alphabet in block script. Or, print copies of the uppercase alphabet in a plain font and have students glue it to the left side of the page. Then, have students identify the parallel and perpendicular lines in the letters using two different colors of highlighters.

Parallel and Perpendicular Lines

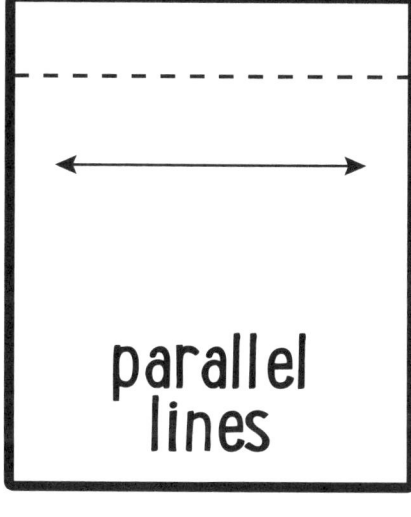

parallel lines

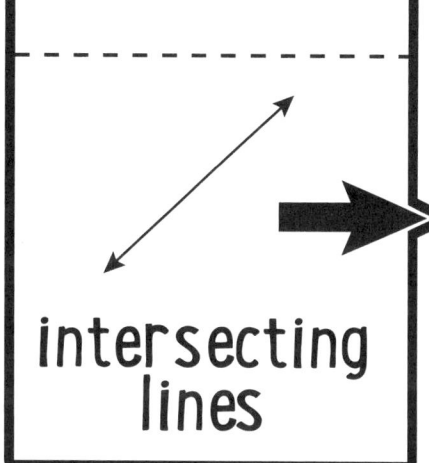

intersecting lines

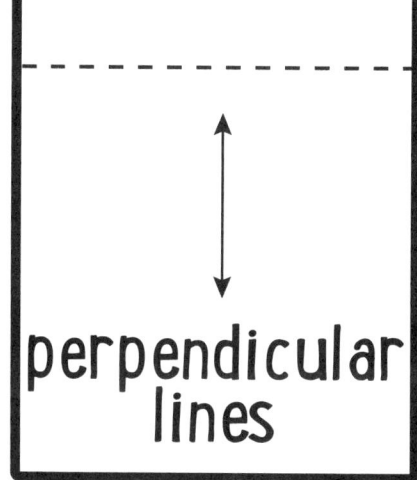

perpendicular lines

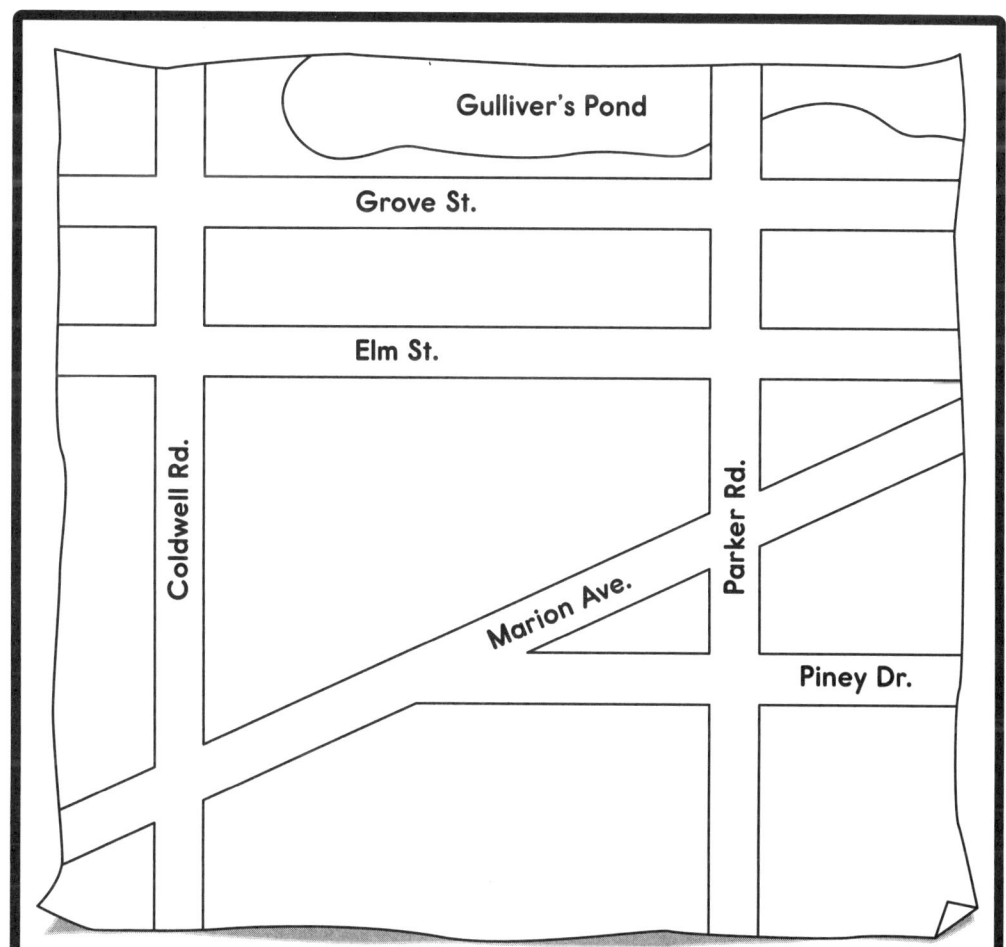

Key
- intersecting lines
- parallel lines
- perpendicular lines

Introduction to Angles

Introduction

Draw students' attention to the clock. Say several times of day and have students show the position of the minute and hour hands with their arms. Discuss how students quickly understand a quarter hour, half hour, and three-quarters of an hour, guiding them to notice the position of the minute hand.

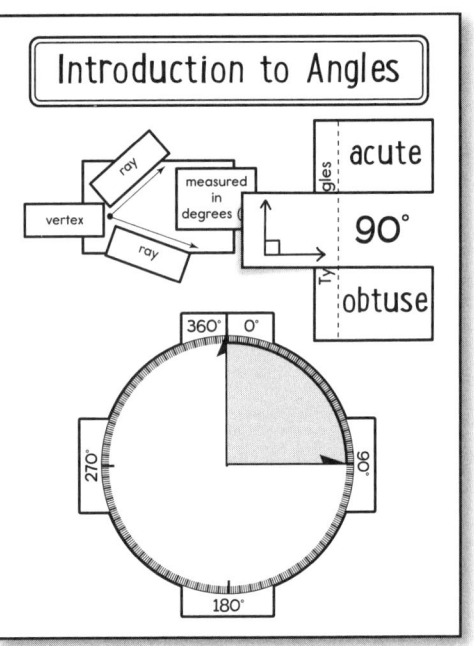

Creating the Notebook Page

Guide students through the following steps to complete the right-hand page in their notebooks.

1. Add a Table of Contents entry for the Introduction to Angles pages.

2. Cut out the title and glue it to the top of the page.

3. Cut out the angle and the vocabulary words. Glue the angle to the top-left side of the page. Discuss the parts of an angle. Glue the *vertex* and *ray* labels to the angle to label each part. Glue the *measured in* piece near the interior of the angle.

4. Cut out both circle pieces. Cut on the solid line from the outside to the center of each circle. With the slits aligned, place the shaded circle behind the white circle. Begin to turn the shaded circle so that it overlaps the front of the white circle. Glue or tape the tabs to the bottom half of the page so that the arrow points up.

5. Point out that each small mark on the white circle measures 1° of a circle. Have students label 0°, 90°, 180°, 270°, and 360° around the outside of the circle. Have students slide the shaded circle around to show different angles such as an acute angle, an obtuse angle, a 30° angle, or an angle measuring more than 180°.

6. Cut out the *Types of Angles* flap book. Cut on the solid lines to create three flaps. Apply glue on the back of the title section and attach it to the top right of the page.

7. On the back of each flap, have students draw an example of each angle. Then, under the flap, have students write the degrees that each type of angle measures. For example, students should write *less than 90°* for acute.

Reflect on Learning

To complete the left-hand page, have students write several times of day to the nearest five minutes. Next, have them draw an analog clock face showing each time. Then, have students describe the type of angle made by the clock hands and give the approximate angle measure for each time.

64

Introduction to Angles

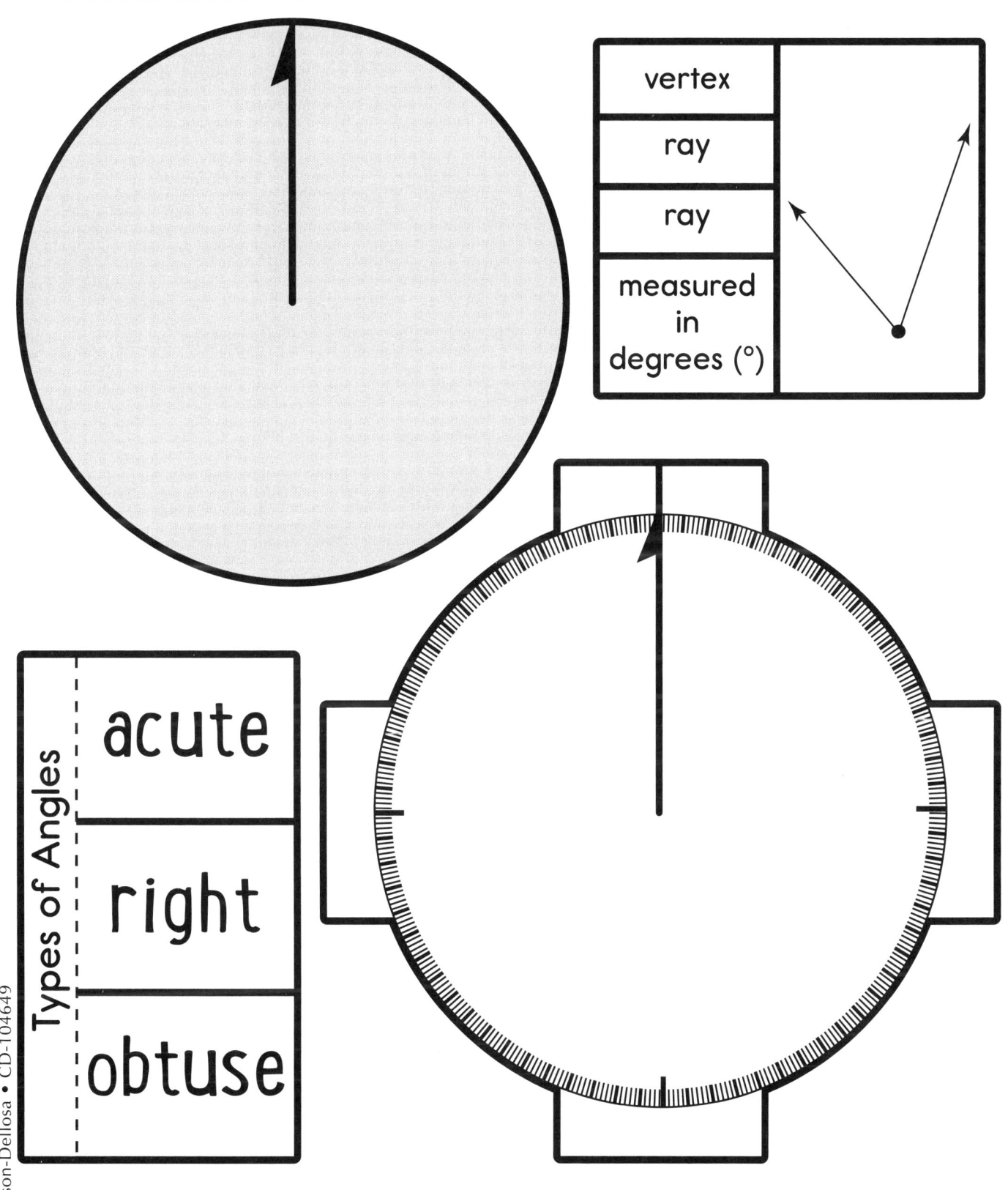

vertex	
ray	
ray	
measured in degrees (°)	

Types of Angles
- acute
- right
- obtuse

Measuring and Drawing Angles

Introduction

Review angles with the class. Say each of the three main types of angles (acute, right, and obtuse) and have students model each with their arms. Then, review the angle measure for each type.

Creating the Notebook Page

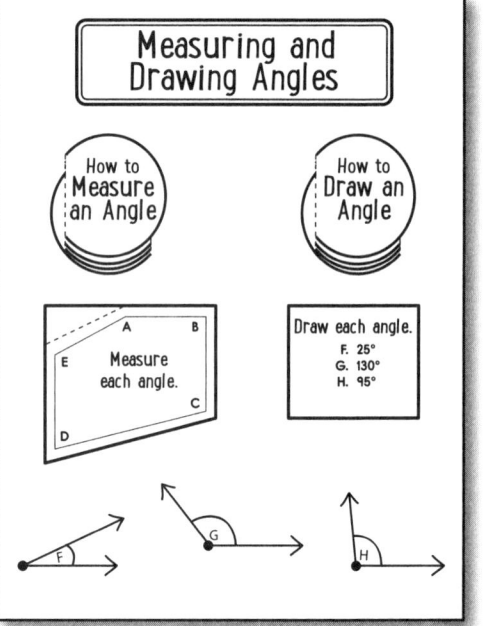

Guide students through the following steps to complete the right-hand page in their notebooks.

1. Add a Table of Contents entry for the Measuring and Drawing Angles pages.

2. Cut out the title and glue it to the top of the page.

3. Cut out the *How to Measure* piece. Starting with the title on top, accordion fold on the dashed lines. Apply glue to the back of the last section. Attach it to the top left of the page.

4. Unfold the accordion. Write a step for measuring an angle on each section, starting at the left. (1. Use a ruler to extend the rays. 2. Align the vertex with the dot on the protractor, called the *origin*. 3. Align the bottom ray with the line on the bottom of the protractor, called the *baseline*. 4. Observe where the ray crosses the numbers, or *scale*. Use the angle type (acute or obtuse) to choose the correct scale.)

5. Repeat step 3 with the *How to Draw* piece and then attach it to the top right of the page.

6. Repeat step 4. (1. Use a straight edge to draw a ray. 2. Align the ray with the origin and the baseline. 3. Make a mark at the correct angle measure, using the correct scale. 4. Draw a straight line connecting the vertex of the ray with the mark you drew.)

7. Cut out the *Measure each angle* and *Draw each angle* pieces. Fold the *Measure* piece along the dashed line. Apply glue to the back of the triangle section and attach it to the left side of the page. Glue the *Draw* piece to the right side of the page, leaving space below.

8. Use a protractor to measure angles A to E on the shape. Write each angle measure under the flap. Then, use a protractor to draw each angle F to H on the page. Label each angle.

Reflect on Learning

To complete the left-hand page, have students switch notebooks with partners. Each partner should draw three angles and write three angle measures between 1° and 179°. Have students return the notebooks. Each student should then measure the angles and draw angles matching the given measures.

Answer Key
A. 152°; B. 90°; C. 104°; D. 76°; E. 119°; F–H. Check students' angles.

Measuring and Drawing Angles

Draw each angle.
- F. 25°
- G. 130°
- H. 95°

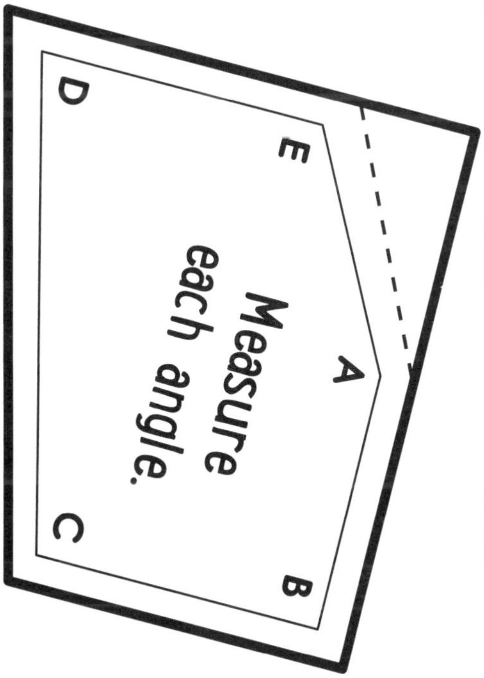

Measure each angle.
(shape with vertices D, E, A, B, C)

How to Measure an Angle

How to Draw an Angle

Finding Unknown Angle Measures

Each student will need three brass paper fasteners to complete this page.

Introduction

Review measuring angles. Have students work with partners. On a sheet of paper, one partner should draw a straight line. The other partner should draw a second straight line to create an angle of any size. The first partner should then use a protractor to measure the drawn angle. Have partners switch roles and repeat.

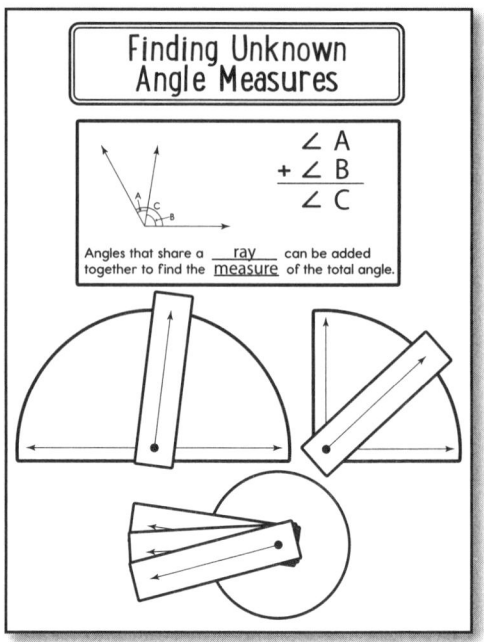

Creating the Notebook Page

Guide students through the following steps to complete the right-hand page in their notebooks.

1. Add a Table of Contents entry for the Finding Unknown Angle Measures pages.

2. Cut out the title and glue it to the top of the page.

3. Cut out the explanation piece and glue it below the title.

4. Use a yellow colored pencil to shade in angle *A*. Use a blue colored pencil to shade in angle *B*. Use a green colored pencil to outline angle *C*. Then, fill in the blanks to complete the explanation. (Angles that share a **ray** can be added together to find the **measure** of the total angle.) Then, name the angles to complete the addition sentence (∠A + ∠B =∠C).

5. Cut out the half circle piece and an arrow. Place the arrow on top of the half circle and press a brass paper fastener through the dots to attach the pieces. It may be helpful to prepunch the hole in each piece separately before connecting them. Glue the half circle to the page. Do not press the brass paper fastener through the notebook page.

6. Discuss how the measure of the total angle for the half circle is always 180°. Then, move the arrow and measure the two angles created by the ray to prove that their measures add up to 180°. Repeat with the arrow in a different position.

7. Repeat steps 5 and 6 with the quarter circle and an arrow. Then, experiment with the ray to show that the two angles created always add up to 90°.

8. Repeat steps 5 and 6 with the circle and three arrows. Then, experiment with the rays to show that the two angles created always add up to the measure of the large angle.

Reflect on Learning

To complete the left-hand page, have students explain in their own words how the additive nature of angle measures is related to what they learned about angles in a circle. Then, have students describe the relationship between additive angle measures and angles such as 90°, 180°, 270°, and 360°.

Finding Unknown Angle Measures

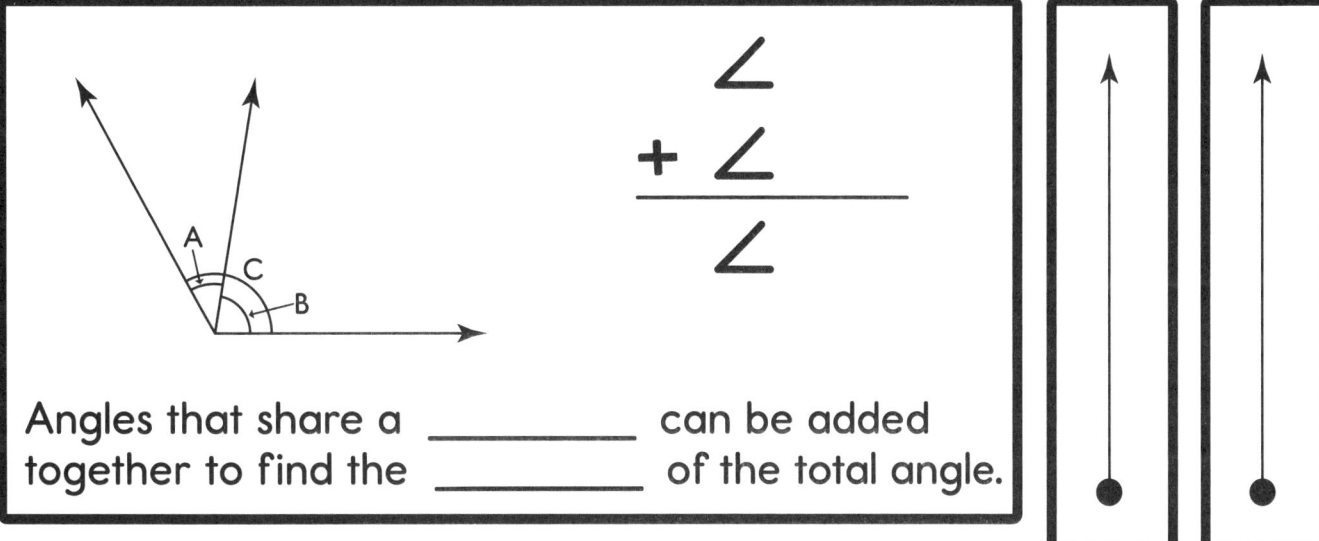

Angles that share a _____ can be added together to find the _____ of the total angle.

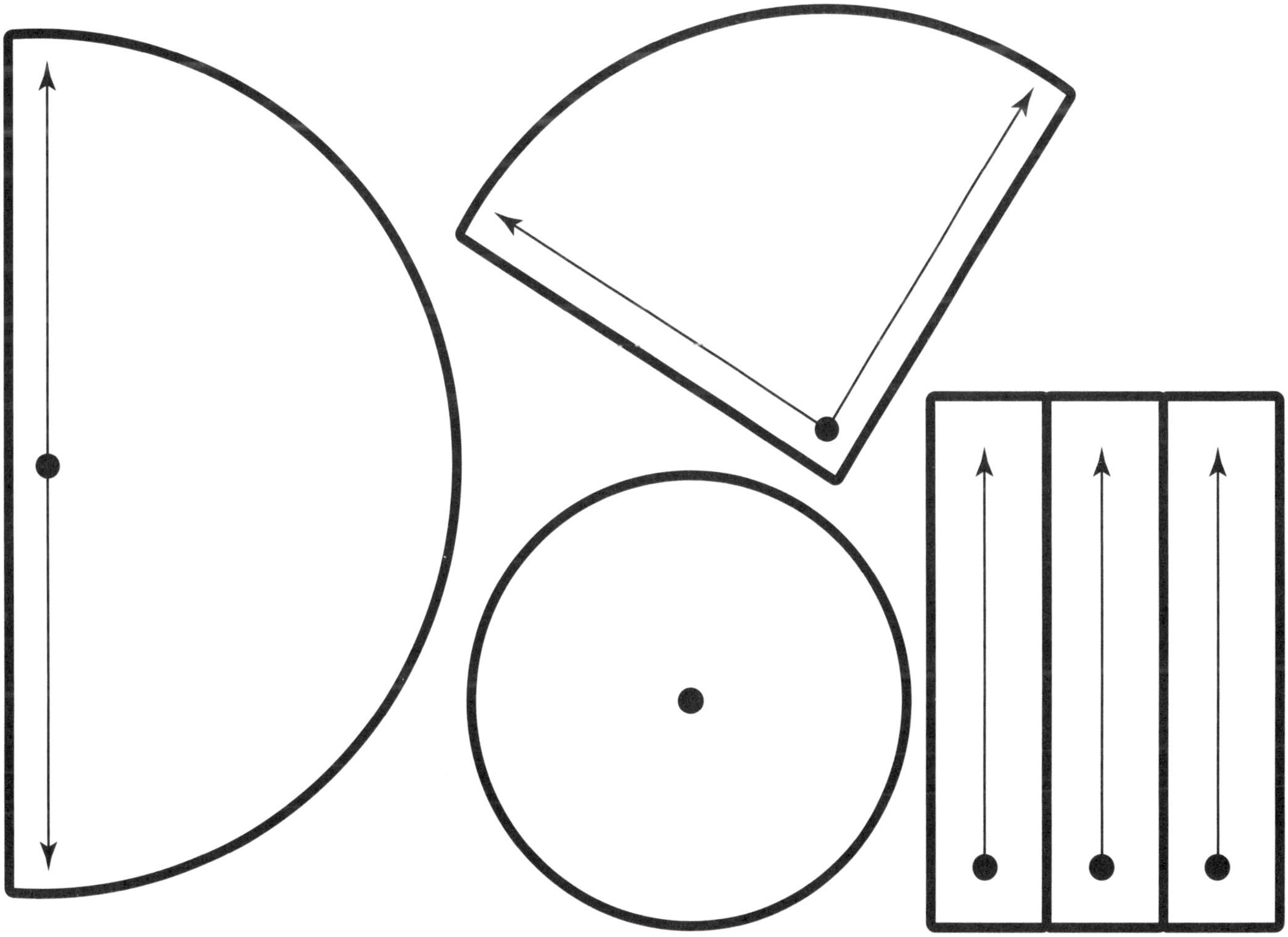

Finding Unknown Angle Measures

Classifying Polygons

Introduction

As a class, create a list of polygons on the board. Have students work in small groups. Have each group decide on a way to organize the polygons in the list into groups. Allow each group to share their categories with the class. Discuss how there are many different ways to group polygons.

Creating the Notebook Page

Guide students through the following steps to complete the right-hand page in their notebooks.

1. Add a Table of Contents entry for the Classifying Polygons pages.

2. Cut out the title and glue it to the top of the page.

3. Cut out the envelope. Fold the tabs and rectangular flap along the dashed lines. Apply glue to the tabs and glue them to the flap to create a pocket. Fold down the triangle to close the envelope. Apply glue to the back of the envelope and attach it to the bottom left of the page.

4. Cut out the long strips. Glue one below the title. Glue the other about halfway down the page.

5. Use a pencil or pen to continue the vertical lines on each strip to create two three-column charts.

6. Cut out the polygons. Write the name of each polygon on the back of each shape.

7. Sort the polygons into the top chart. Record the names of the polygons on the page in the correct columns.

8. Repeat step 7 with the bottom chart. Store the polygons in the envelope when not using them.

Reflect on Learning

To complete the left-hand page, have students re-create the two charts from the right-hand page. Then, have students draw at least one new shape to add to each column.

Classifying Polygons

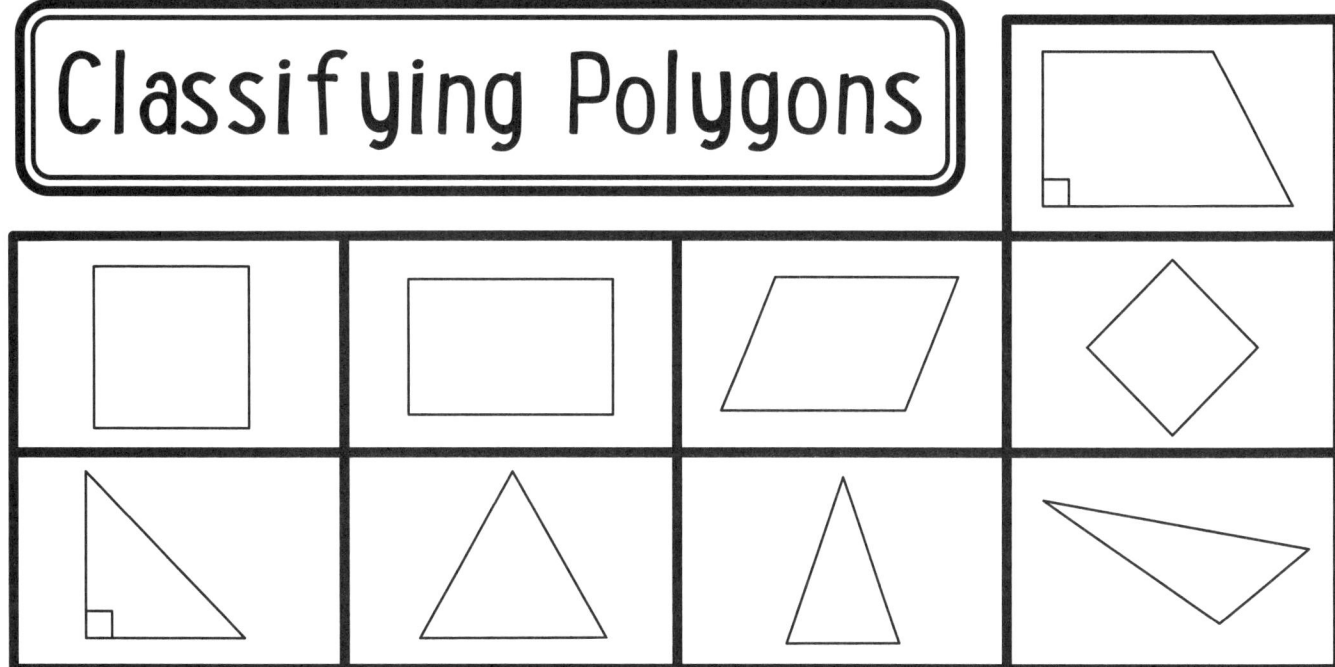

No Parallel Lines	One Pair of Parallel Lines	More Than One Pair of Parallel Lines
No Right Angles	One Right Angle	More Than One Right Angle

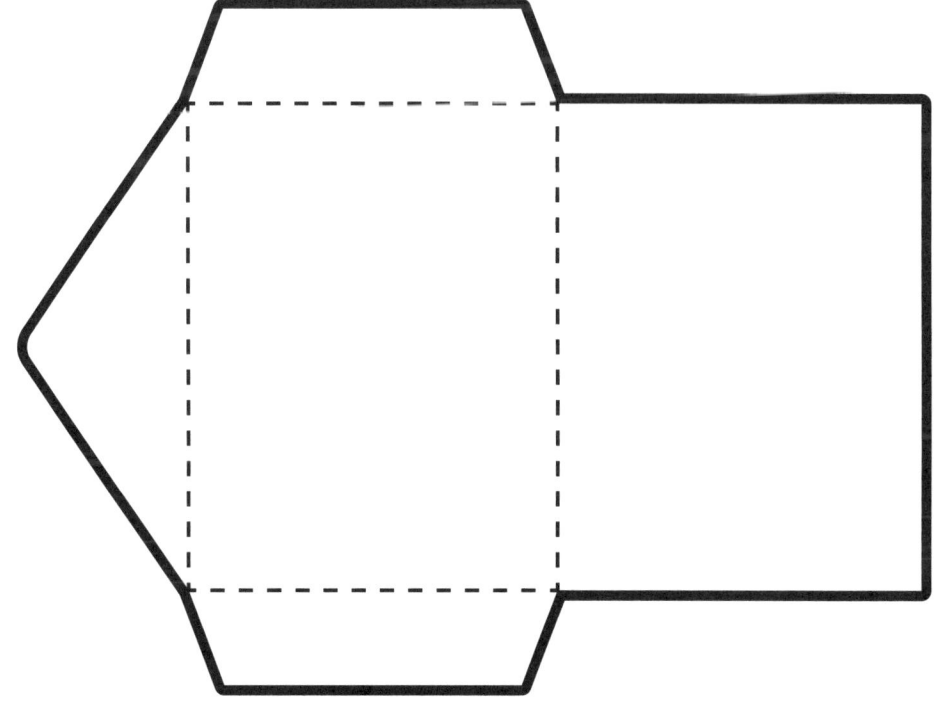

Symmetry

Introduction

Discuss the term *mirror image*. Have students work in small groups to come up with a definition. Have each group share its definition. Then, come up with a final definition as a class and write it on the board.

Creating the Notebook Page

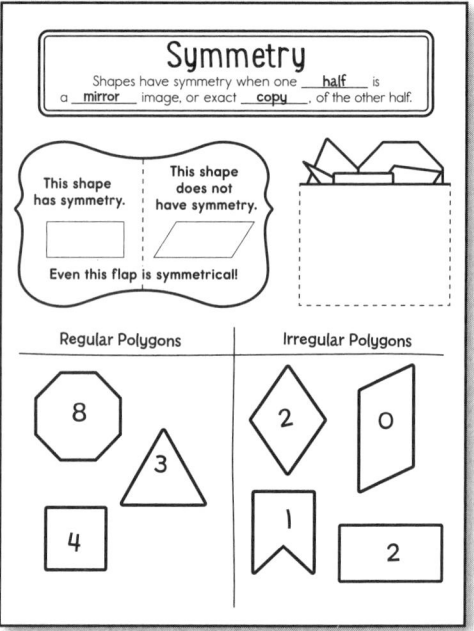

Guide students through the following steps to complete the right-hand page in their notebooks.

1. Add a Table of Contents entry for the Symmetry pages.

2. Cut out the title and glue it to the top of the page.

3. Complete the explanation of symmetry. (Shapes have symmetry when one **half** is a **mirror** image, or exact **copy**, of the other half.)

4. Cut out the explanation piece. Fold it in half along the dashed line. Apply glue to the back of the left side of the piece and attach it to the top left side of the page.

5. Read each side of the explanation piece. Draw the lines of symmetry on the symmetrical example piece. Discuss how shapes can have one or more lines of symmetry. Fold the piece itself in half to test its line of symmetry. Discuss why it is not symmetrical from top to bottom as well.

6. Cut out the pocket. Fold the tabs and rectangular flap in along the dashed lines. Apply glue to the tabs and glue them to the flap to create a pocket. Apply glue to the back of the pocket and attach it to the top right side of the page.

7. Cut out all of the shapes. Experiment and fold each piece to find all of its lines of symmetry (if any). Draw the line or lines of symmetry on each piece. Write the total number of lines of symmetry on the back of each piece.

8. Draw a T-chart on the page. Label one side Regular Polygons. Label the other side Irregular Polygons. Sort the shapes. Trace each shape and write the number of lines of symmetry in the center. Look for patterns in the number of lines of symmetry.

Reflect on Learning

To complete the left-hand page, have students write any patterns they noticed in the number of lines of symmetry for regular polygons. Then, students should predict the number of lines of symmetry for a regular decagon (10 sides) and dodecagon (12 sides).

Symmetry

Shapes have symmetry when one _____ is a _____ image, or exact _____, of the other half.

This shape does not have symmetry.

This shape has symmetry.

Even this flap is symmetrical!

Symmetry   73

Transformations

Introduction

Have students stand behind their desks. Ask them to *slide*. Then, discuss how students demonstrated that word. Next, ask students to *turn*. Discuss how students demonstrated that word. Have students choose partners. Then, ask partners to work together to demonstrate *reflect*. Discuss how students demonstrated that word.

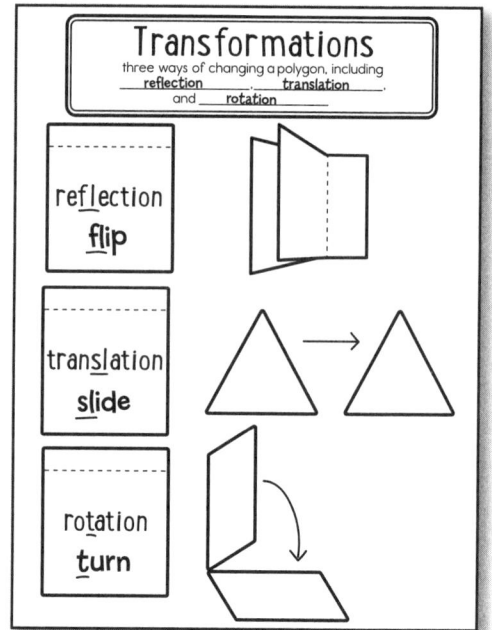

Creating the Notebook Page

Guide students through the following steps to complete the right-hand page in their notebooks.

1. Add a Table of Contents entry for the Transformations pages.

2. Cut out the title and glue it to the top of the page.

3. Complete the definition of *transformation* (three ways of changing a polygon, including a **reflection**, **translation**, and **rotation**).

4. Cut out the three flaps. Apply glue to the back of each narrow section and attach the flaps along the left side of the page.

5. On each flap, write the simple term under the vocabulary word (*flip, slide,* and *turn*). Then, underline or highlight the *fl* in *reflection* and *flip*, the *sl* in *translation* and *slide*, and the *t* in *rotation* and *turn* to provide a simple way to remember each vocabulary word.

6. Under each flap, write a simple definition for each vocabulary word.

7. Cut out the two trapezoid pieces. Glue the non-flap trapezoid beside the *reflection* flap. Apply glue to the back of the rectangular section of the other trapezoid. Attach it to the page so that the flap overlaps the original trapezoid exactly. Fold over the piece and color the sides of the trapezoid that face each other the same color.

8. Cut out the triangles. Glue one triangle beside the *translation* flap. Glue the other triangle to the right. Color each triangle the same color. Draw an arrow to show the slide.

9. Cut out the parallelograms. Glue one parallelogram beside the rotation flap. Glue the second parallelogram so that it shows rotation around one of the corners. The corners should be touching. Color each parallelogram the same color. Draw an arrow to show the rotation.

Reflect on Learning

To complete the left-hand page, have students each draw a simple shape. Then, the student should draw and label an example of a reflection, translation, and rotation of that shape.

Transformations

three ways of changing a polygon, including

_____ , _____ ,

and _____

| reflection | translation | rotation |

Transformations 75

The Coordinate Plane

Introduction

Display a map with at least two prominent points of interest. Ask students to give directions to partners for getting from one point to the other. Then, as a class, discuss how easy or difficult it was to be clear when giving directions. Explain that mathematicians have developed a way to give precise directions to a point in space.

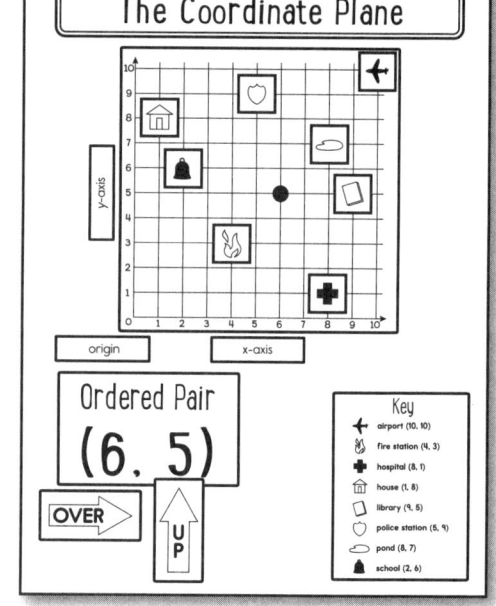

Creating the Notebook Page

Guide students through the following steps to complete the right-hand page in their notebooks.

1. Add a Table of Contents entry for the The Coordinate Plane pages.

2. Cut out the title and glue it to the top of the page.

3. Cut out the coordinate plane piece and the three labels. Apply glue to the back of the coordinate plane and glue it below the title.

4. Label the numbers on each axis, including the origin. Then, glue the three labels around the coordinate plane to label each important part.

5. Cut out the *Ordered Pair* piece and the two arrow pieces. Glue the ordered pair piece to the bottom left of the page, leaving space below it for the arrows. Glue the *Over* arrow under the 6 and glue the *Up* arrow below the 5.

6. Discuss how the ordered pair describes a specific point on the plane. Starting at the origin, count 6 to the right along the x-axis. Then, count 5 up along the y-axis. Plot the point.

7. Cut out the key. Glue it to the right of the ordered pair, below the coordinate plane.

8. Cut out the symbols. Using the ordered pairs on the key, glue each symbol to the correct place on the coordinate plane.

Reflect on Learning

To complete the left-hand page, have students draw and label their own coordinate planes, with each axis going to at least 10. Then, students should draw each of the eight symbols on their grids and create matching keys with coordinate pairs to identify each point of interest. Students may add additional points of interest as desired.

The Coordinate Plane

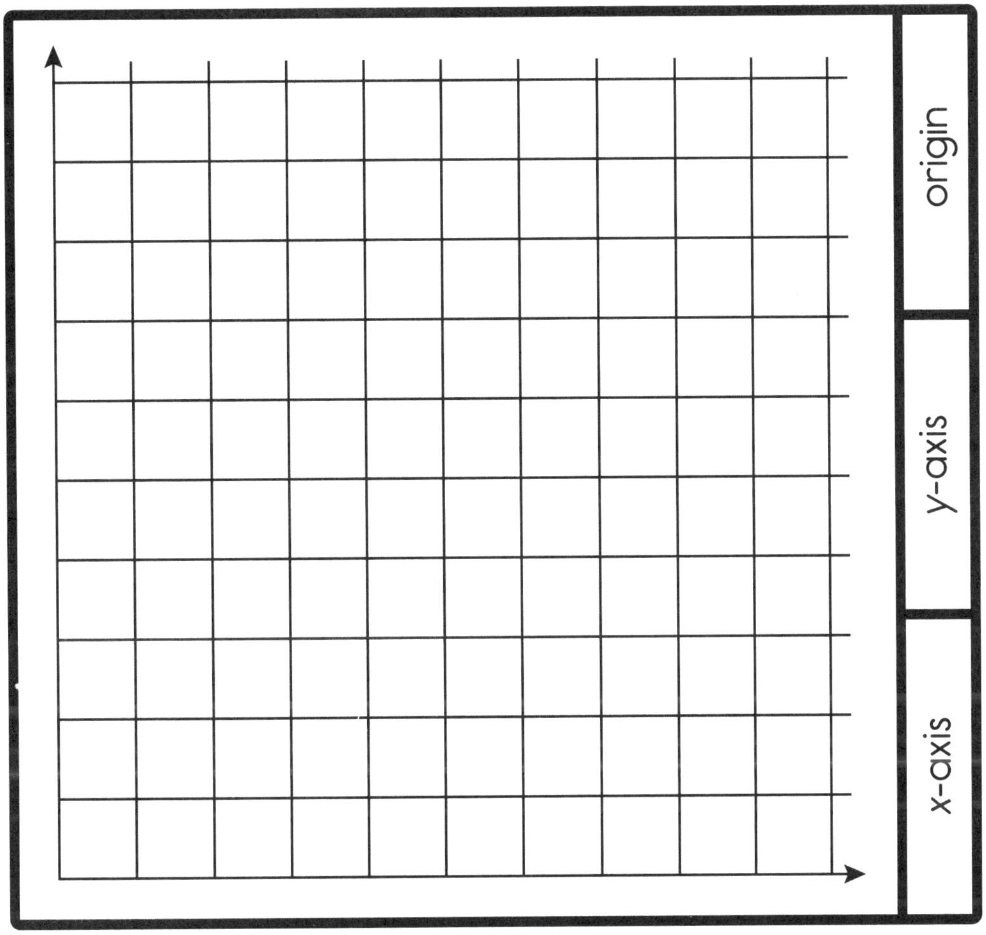

origin

y-axis

x-axis

UP

OVER

Key

 airport (10, 10)

 fire station (4, 3)

 hospital (8, 1)

 house (1, 8)

 library (9, 5)

 police station (5, 9)

 pond (8, 7)

 school (2, 6)

Ordered Pair (6, 5)

Tabs

Cut out each tab and label it. Apply glue to the back of each tab and align it on the outside edge of the page with only the label section showing beyond the edge. Then, fold each tab to seal the page inside.

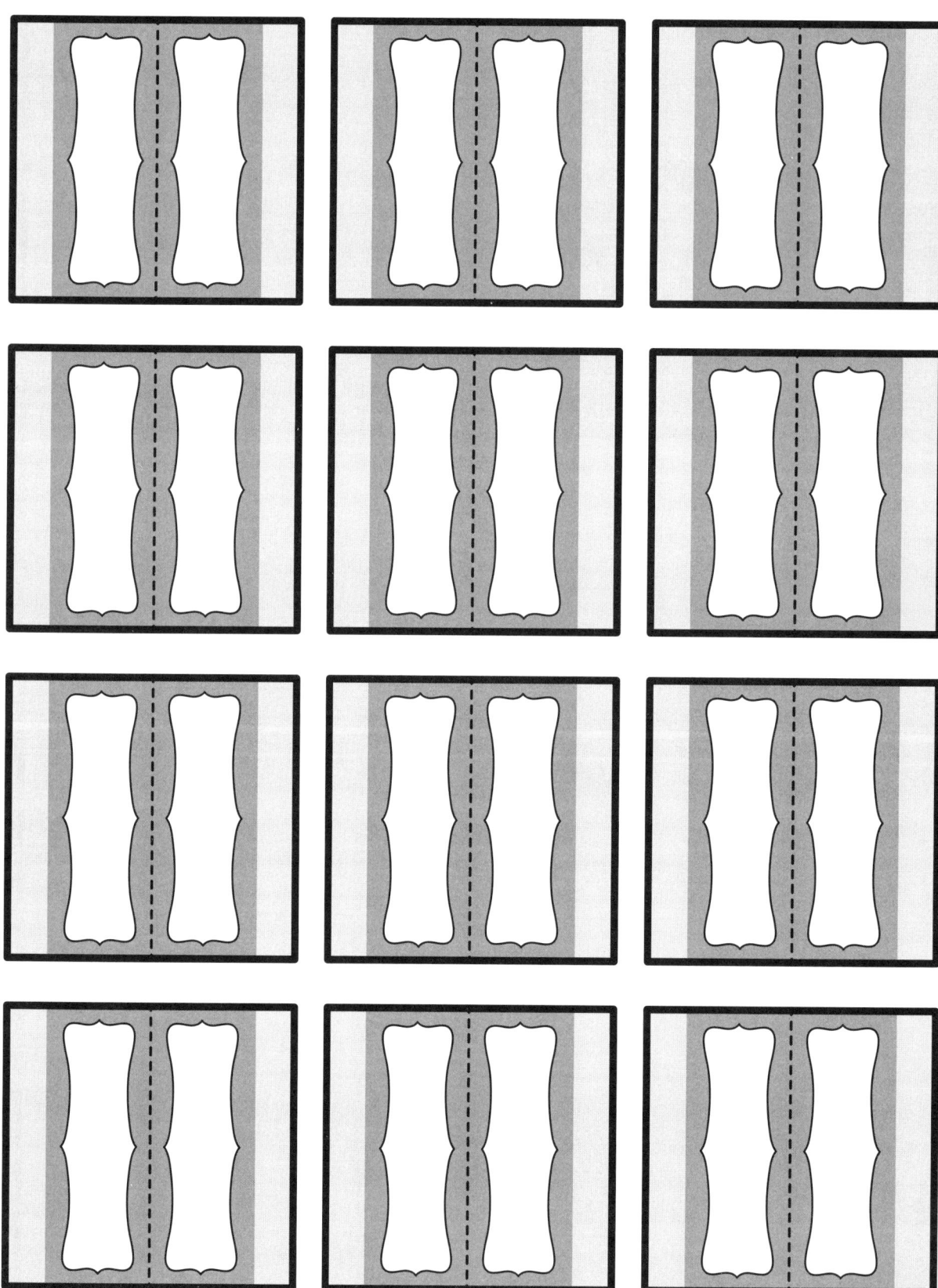

KWL Chart

Cut out the KWL chart and cut on the solid lines to create three separate flaps. Apply glue to the back of the "Topic" section to attach the chart to a notebook page.

Library Pocket

Cut out the library pocket on the solid lines. Fold in the side tabs and apply glue to them before folding up the front of the pocket. Apply glue to the back of the pocket to attach it to a notebook page.

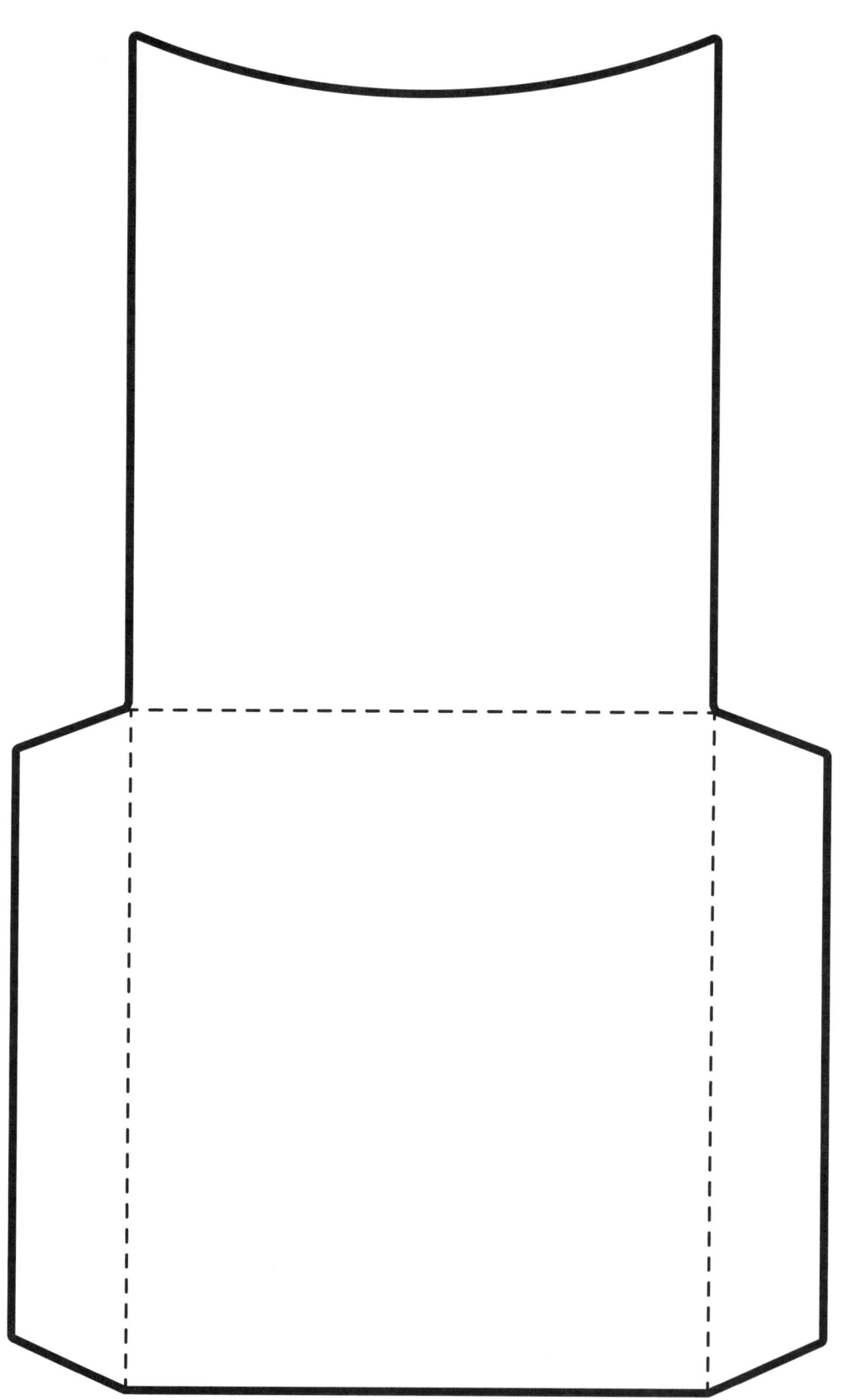

Envelope

Cut out the envelope on the solid lines. Fold in the side tabs and apply glue to them before folding up the rectangular front of the envelope. Fold down the triangular flap to close the envelope. Apply glue to the back of the envelope to attach it to a notebook page.

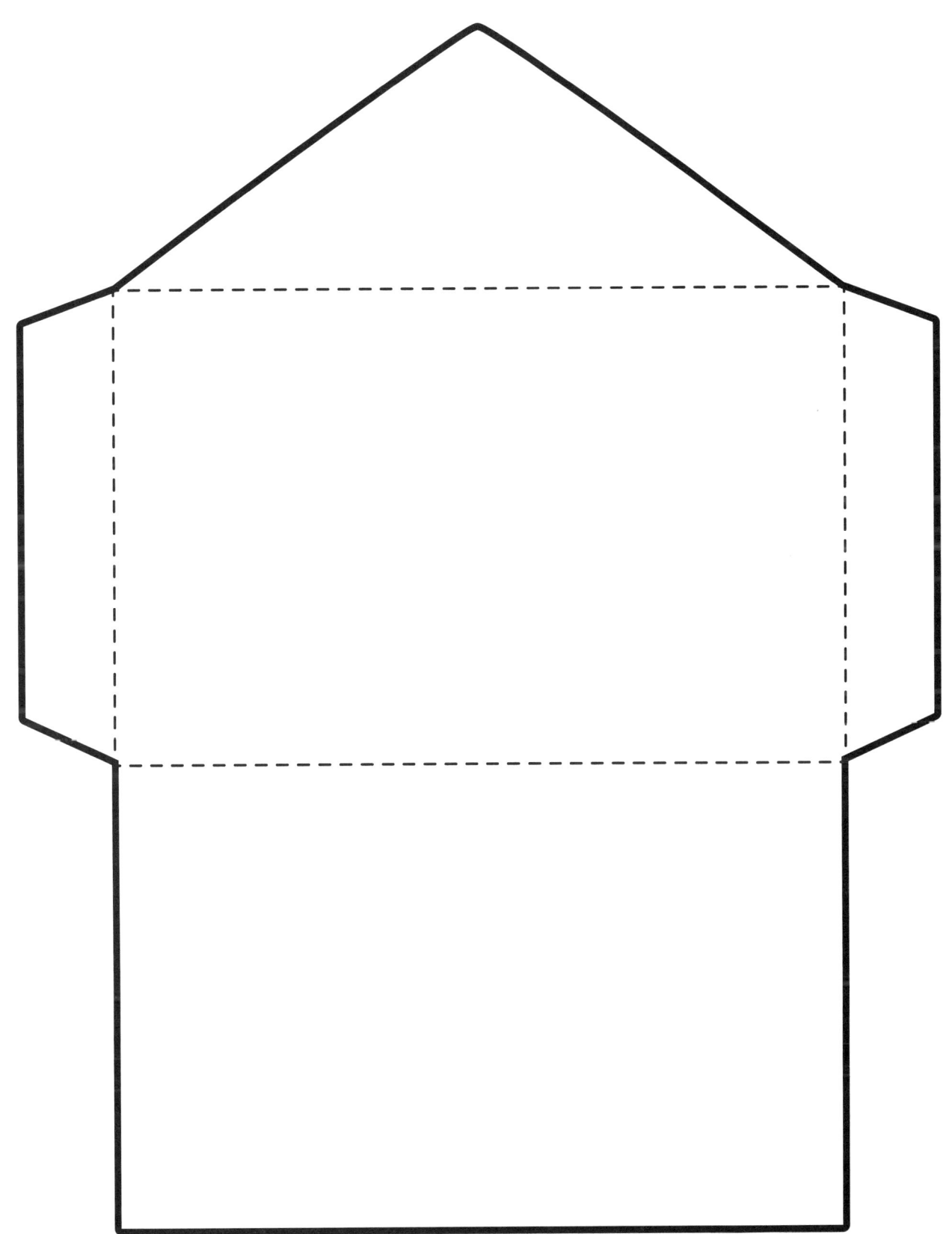

Pocket and Cards

Cut out the pocket on the solid lines. Fold over the front of the pocket. Then, apply glue to the tabs and fold them around the back of the pocket. Apply glue to the back of the pocket to attach it to a notebook page. Cut out the cards and store them in the envelope.

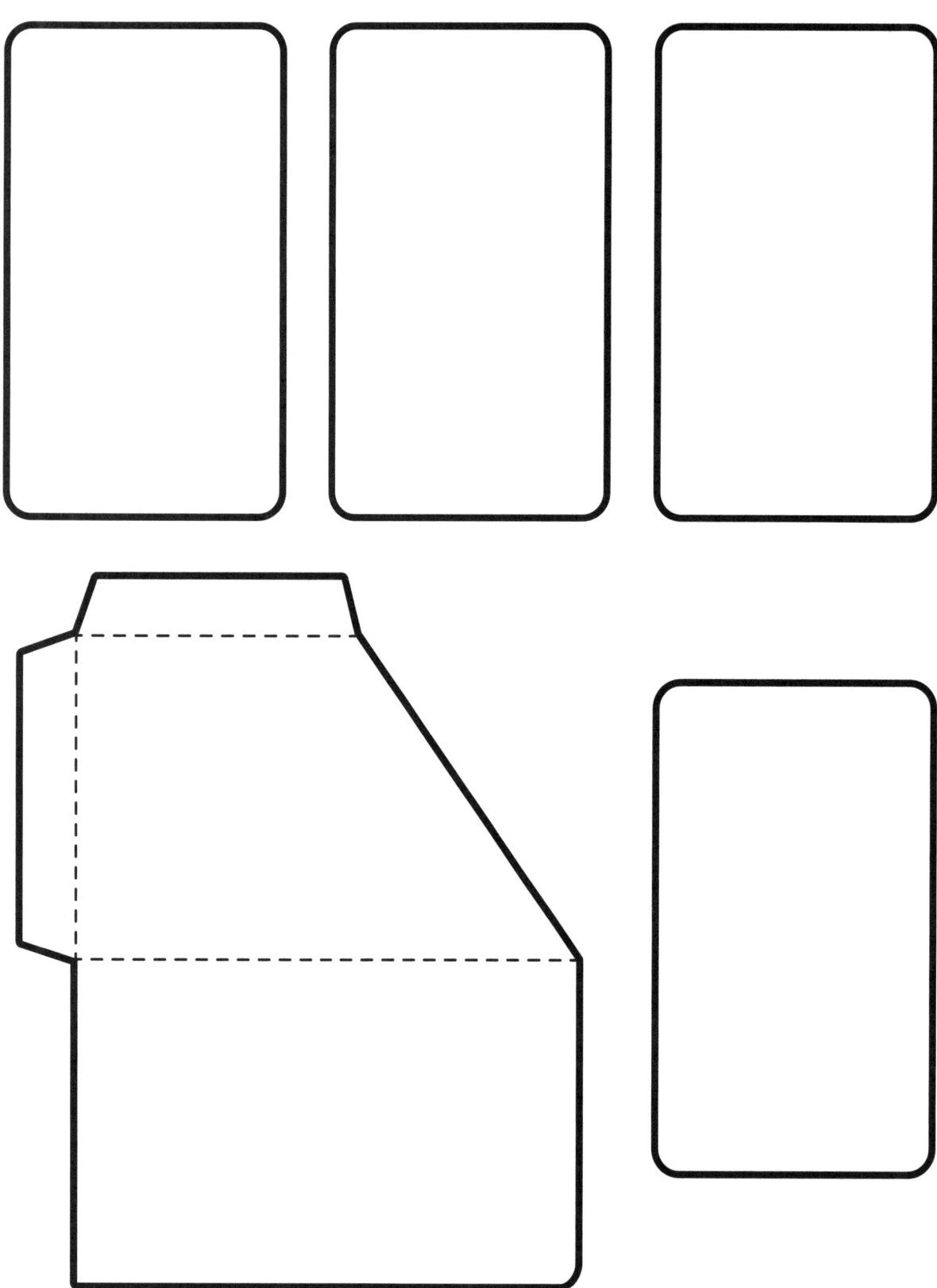

Six-Flap Shutter Fold

Cut out the shutter fold around the outside border. Then, cut on the solid lines to create six flaps. Fold the flaps toward the center. Apply glue to the back of the shutter fold to attach it to a notebook page.

If desired, this template can be modified to create a four-flap shutter fold by cutting off the bottom row. You can also create two three-flap books by cutting it in half down the center line.

Eight-Flap Shutter Fold

Cut out the shutter fold around the outside border. Then, cut on the solid lines to create eight flaps. Fold the flaps toward the center. Apply glue to the back of the shutter fold to attach it to a notebook page.

If desired, this template can be modified to create two four-flap shutter folds by cutting off the bottom two rows. You can also create two four-flap books by cutting it in half down the center line.

Flap Book—Eight Flaps

Cut out the flap book around the outside border. Then, cut on the solid lines to create eight flaps. Apply glue to the back of the center section to attach it to a notebook page.

If desired, this template can be modified to create a six-flap or two four-flap books by cutting off the bottom row or two. You can also create a tall four-flap book by cutting off the flaps on the left side.

Flap Book—Twelve Flaps

Cut out the flap book around the outside border. Then, cut on the solid lines to create 12 flaps. Apply glue to the back of the center section to attach it to a notebook page.

If desired, this template can be modified to create smaller flap books by cutting off any number of rows from the bottom. You can also create a tall flap book by cutting off the flaps on the left side.

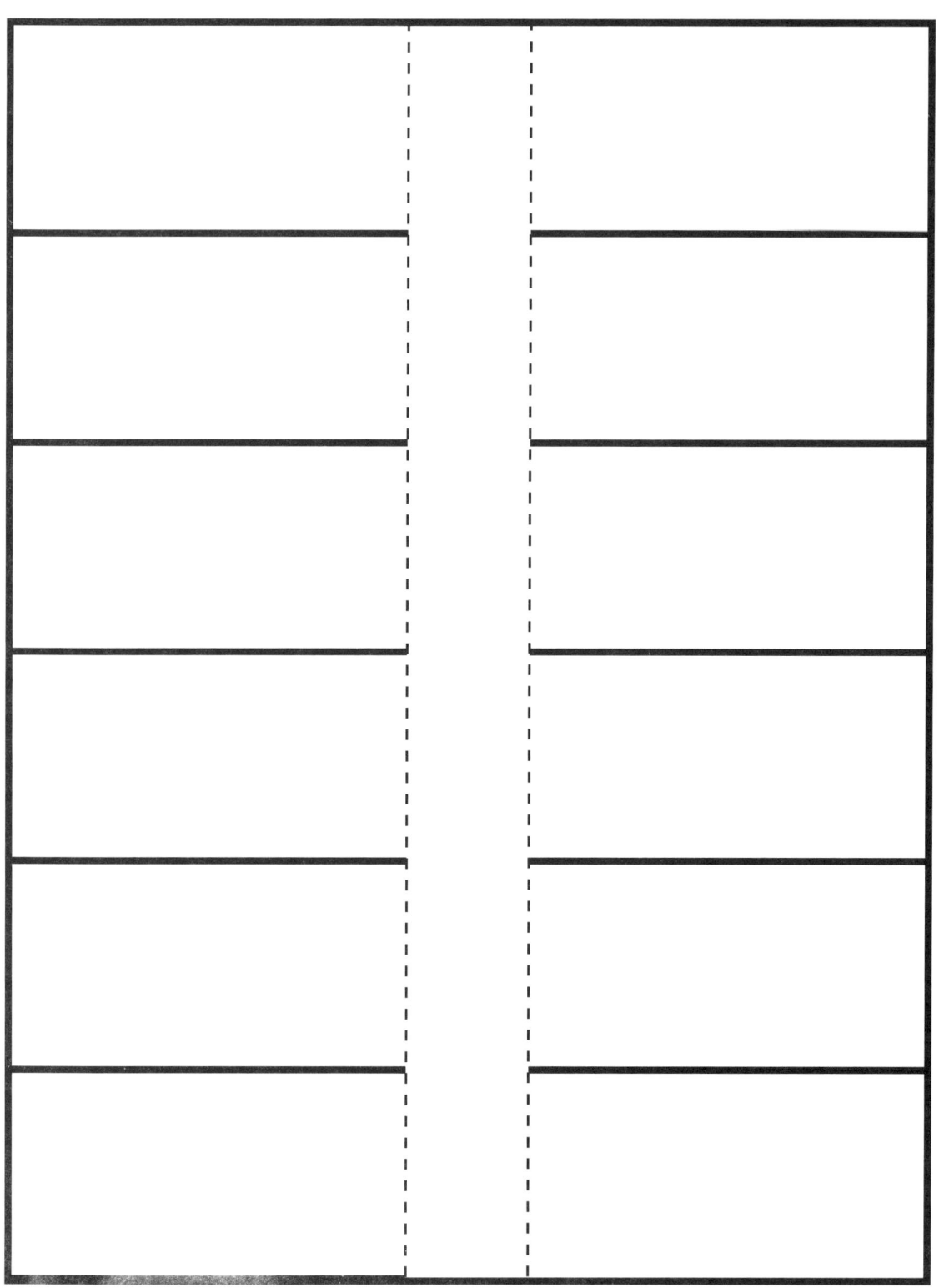

Shaped Flaps

Cut out each shaped flap. Apply glue to the back of the narrow section to attach it to a notebook page.

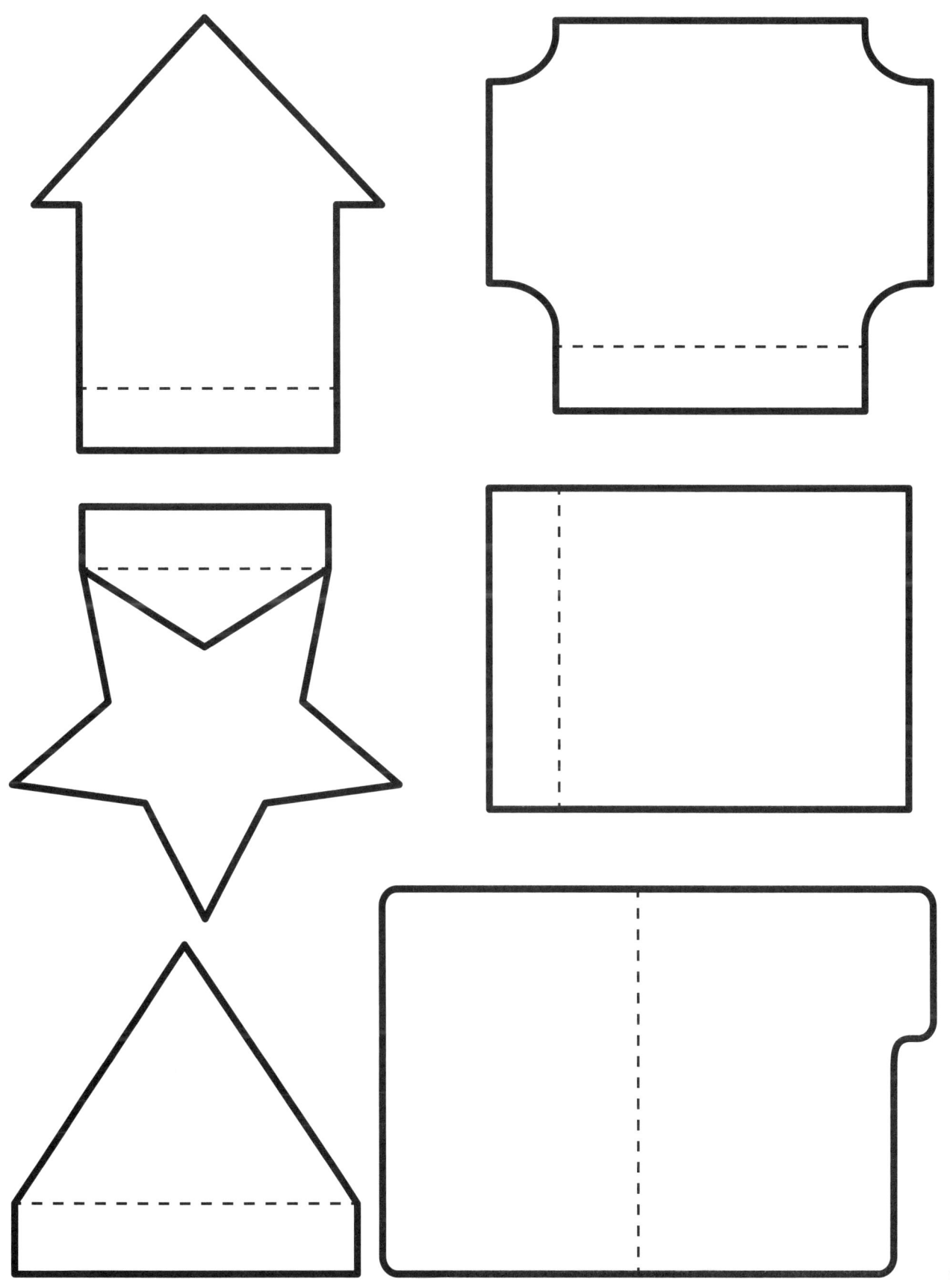

87

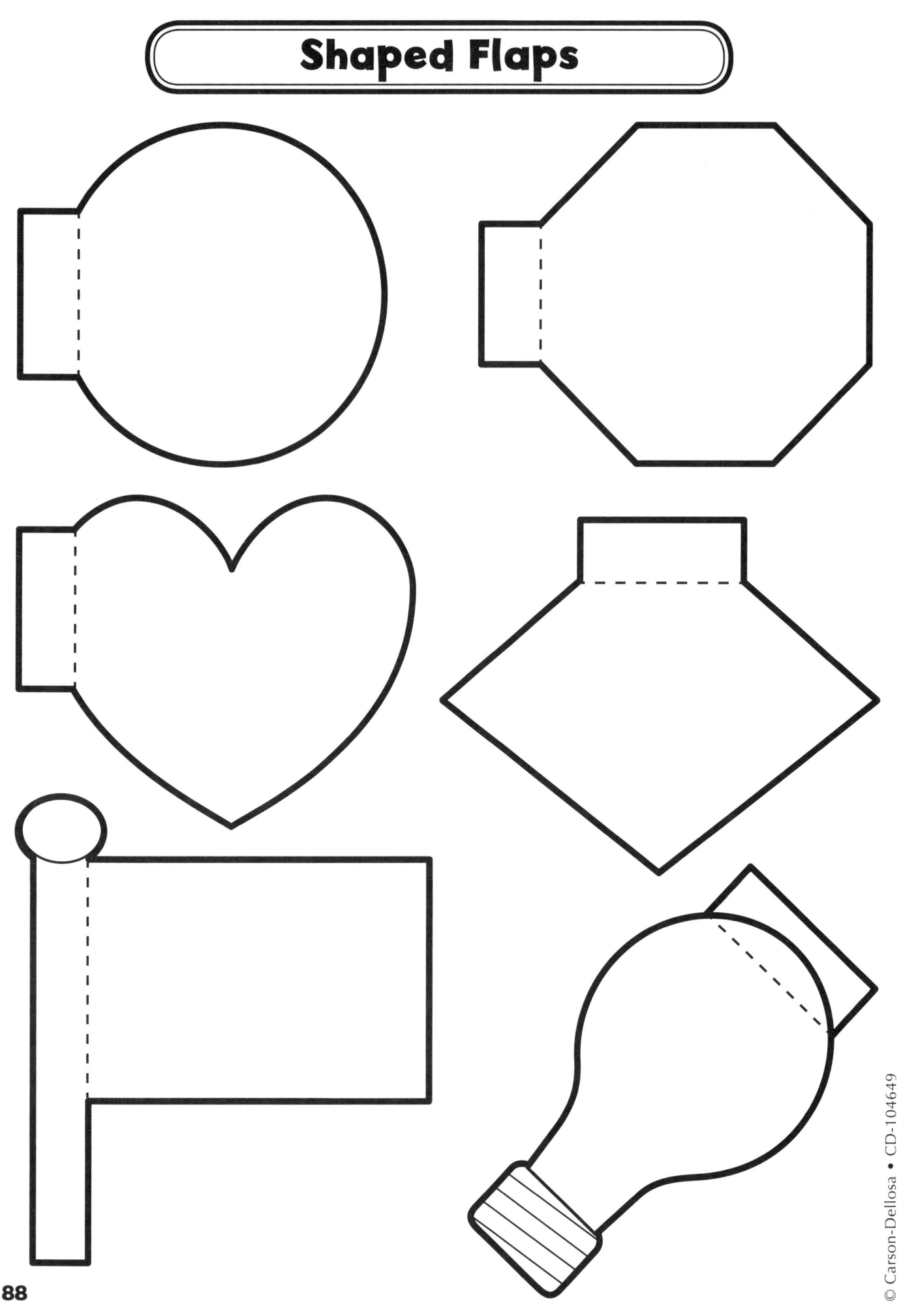

Interlocking Booklet

Cut out the booklet on the solid lines, including the short vertical lines on the top and bottom flaps. Then, fold the top and bottom flaps toward the center, interlocking them using the small vertical cuts. Apply glue to the back of the center panel to attach it to a notebook page.

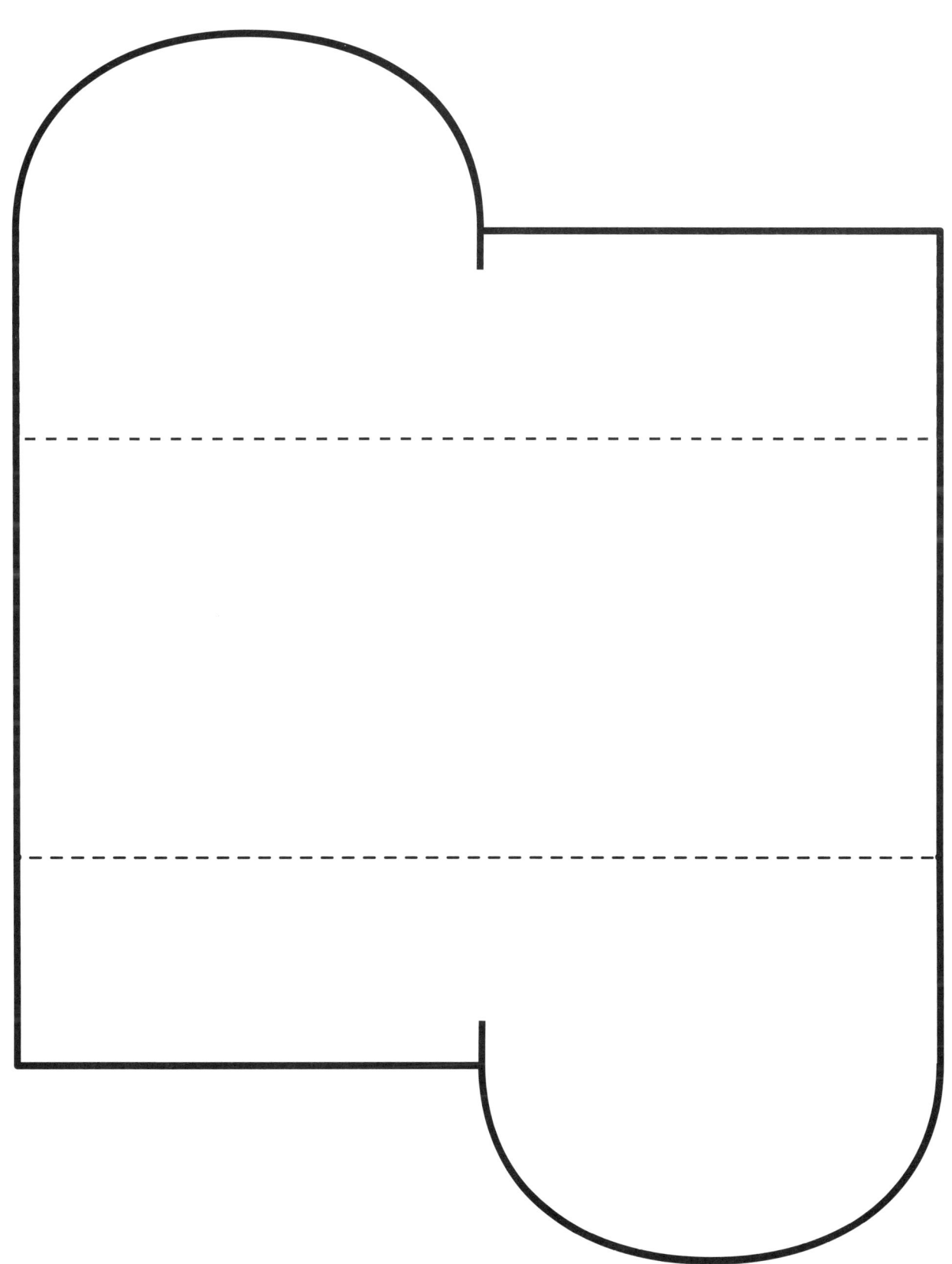

Four-Flap Petal Fold

Cut out the shape on the solid lines. Then, fold the flaps toward the center. Apply glue to the back of the center panel to attach it to a notebook page.

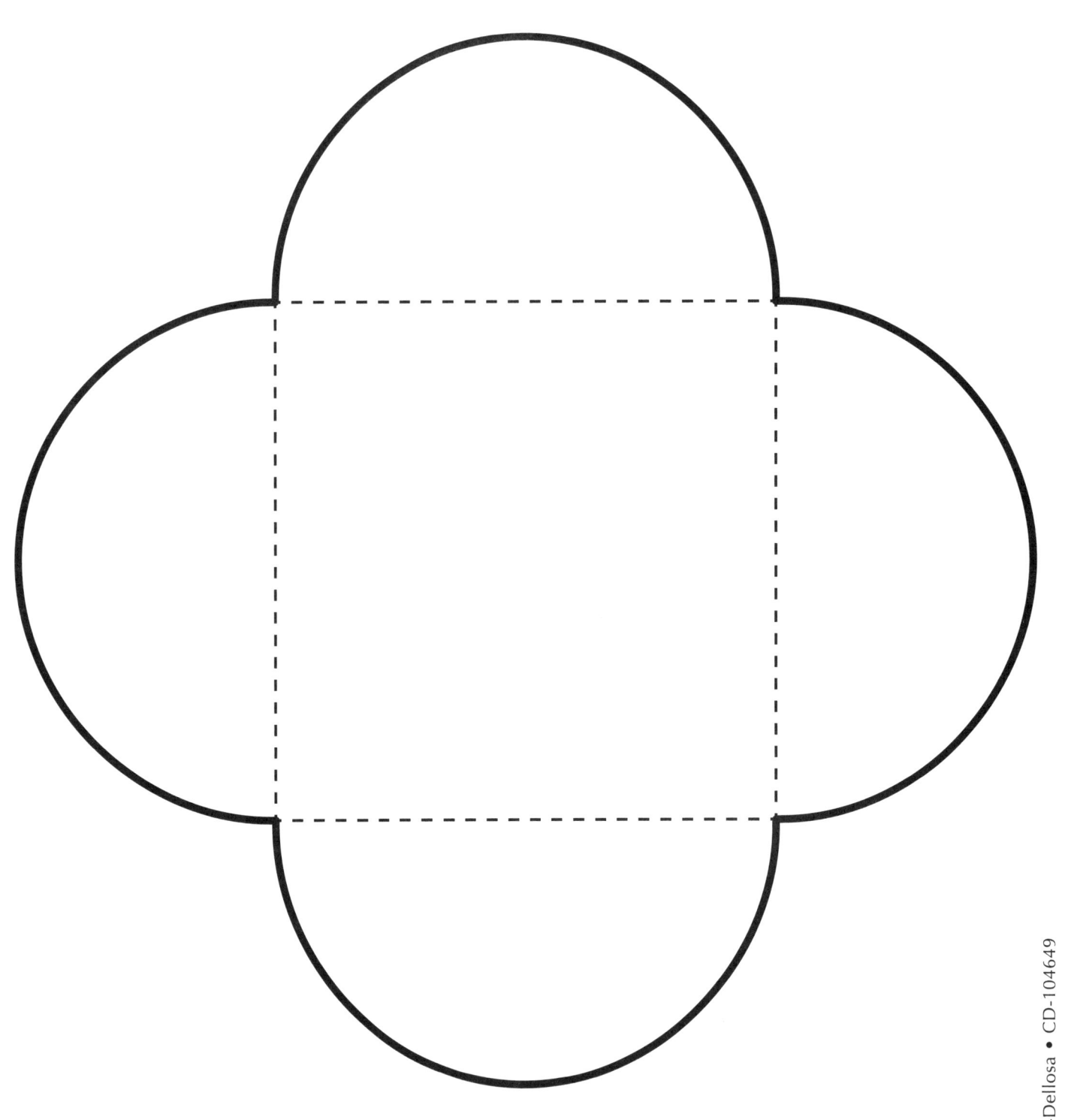

Six-Flap Petal Fold

Cut out the shape on the solid lines. Then, fold the flaps toward the center and back out. Apply glue to the back of the center panel to attach it to a notebook page.

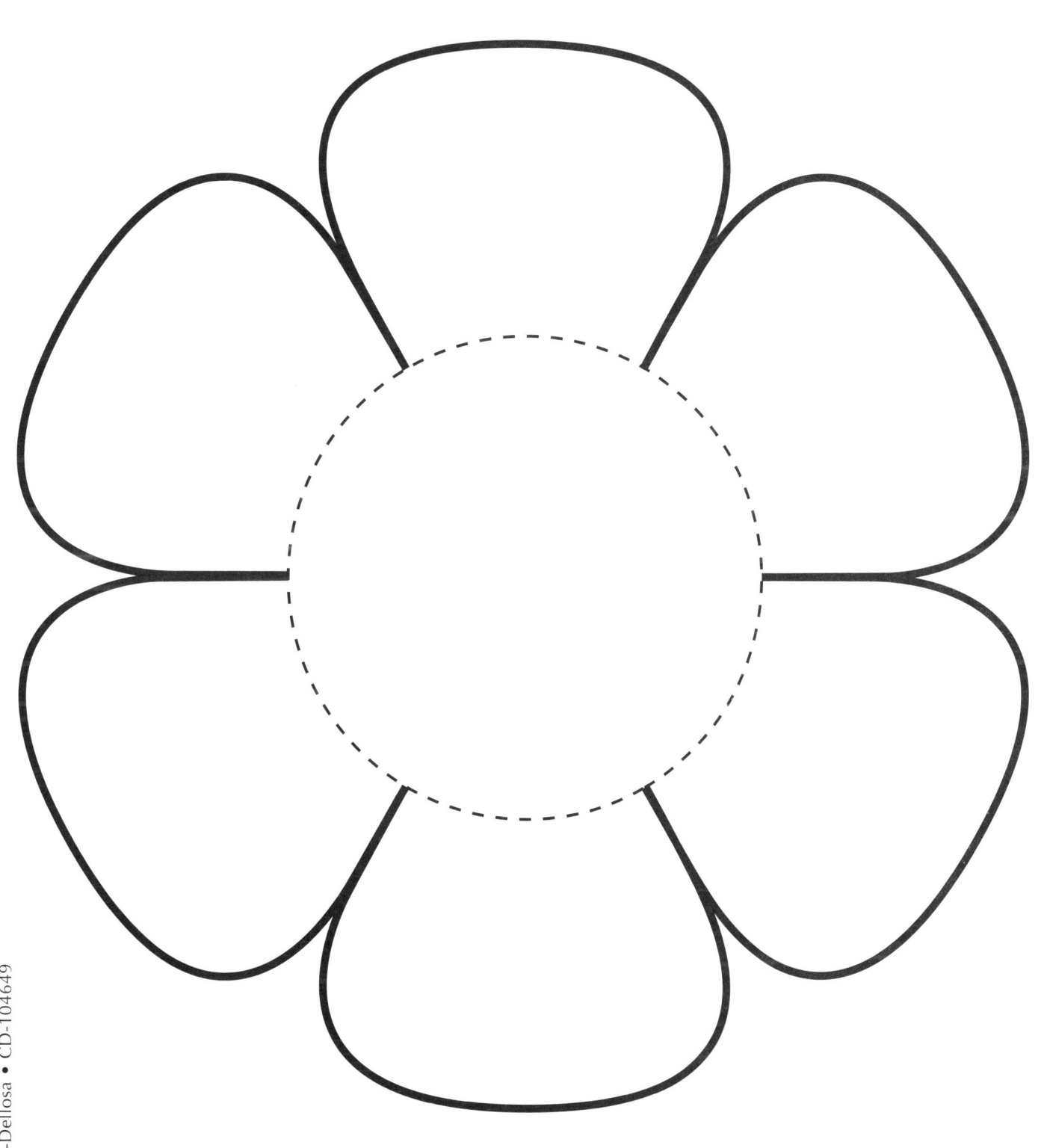

Accordion Folds

Cut out the accordion pieces on the solid lines. Fold on the dashed lines, alternating the fold direction. Apply glue to the back of the last section to attach it to a notebook page.

You may modify the accordion books to have more or fewer pages by cutting off extra pages or by having students glue the first and last panels of two accordion books together.

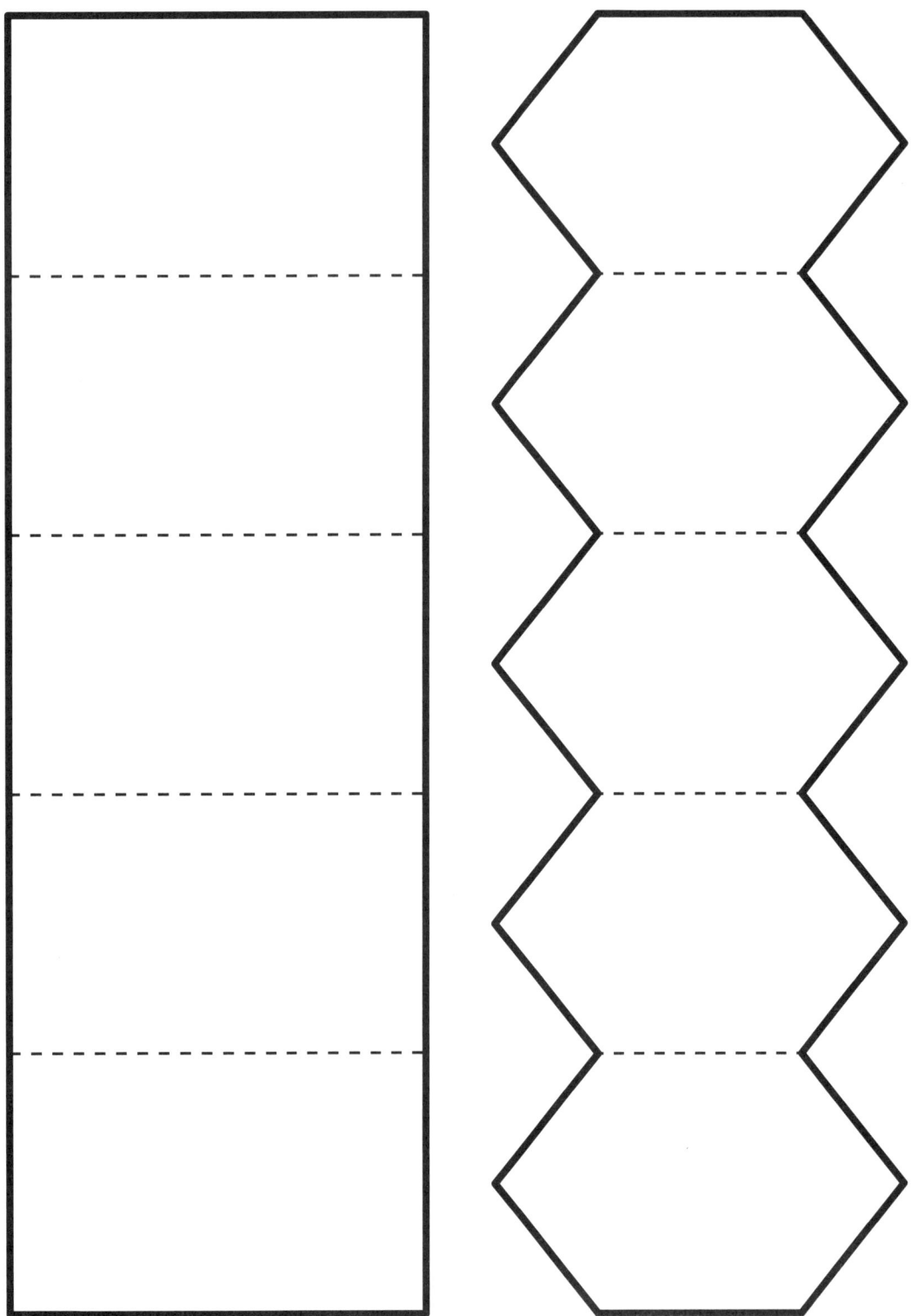

Accordion Folds

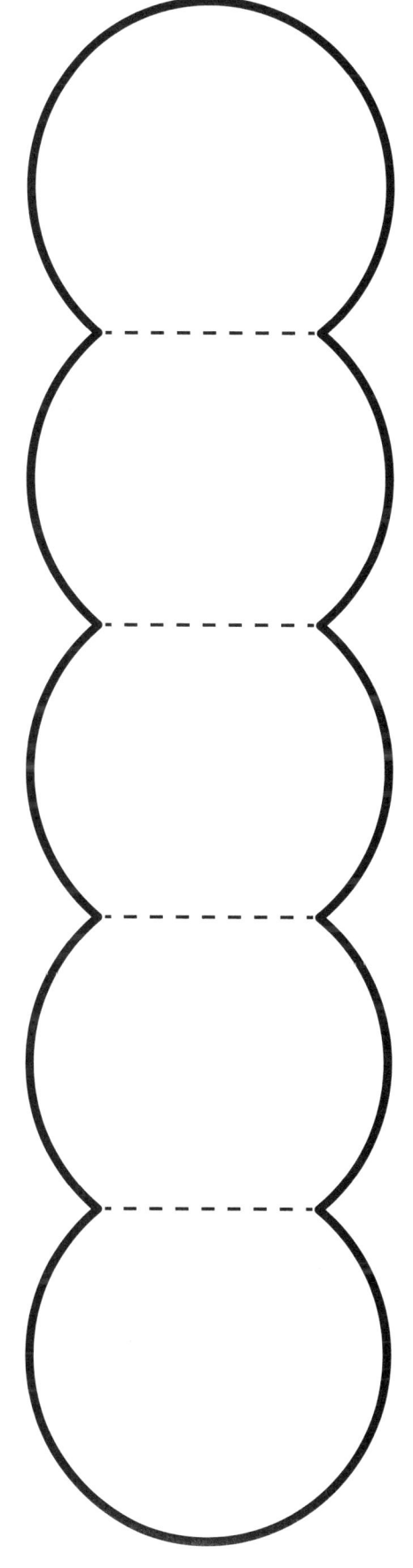

Clamshell Fold

Cut out the clamshell fold on the solid lines. Fold and unfold the piece on the three dashed lines. With the piece oriented so that the folds form an X with a horizontal line through it, pull the left and right sides together at the fold line. Then, keeping the sides touching, bring the top edge down to meet the bottom edge. You should be left with a triangular shape that unfolds into a square. Apply glue to the back of the triangle to attach the clamshell to a notebook page.

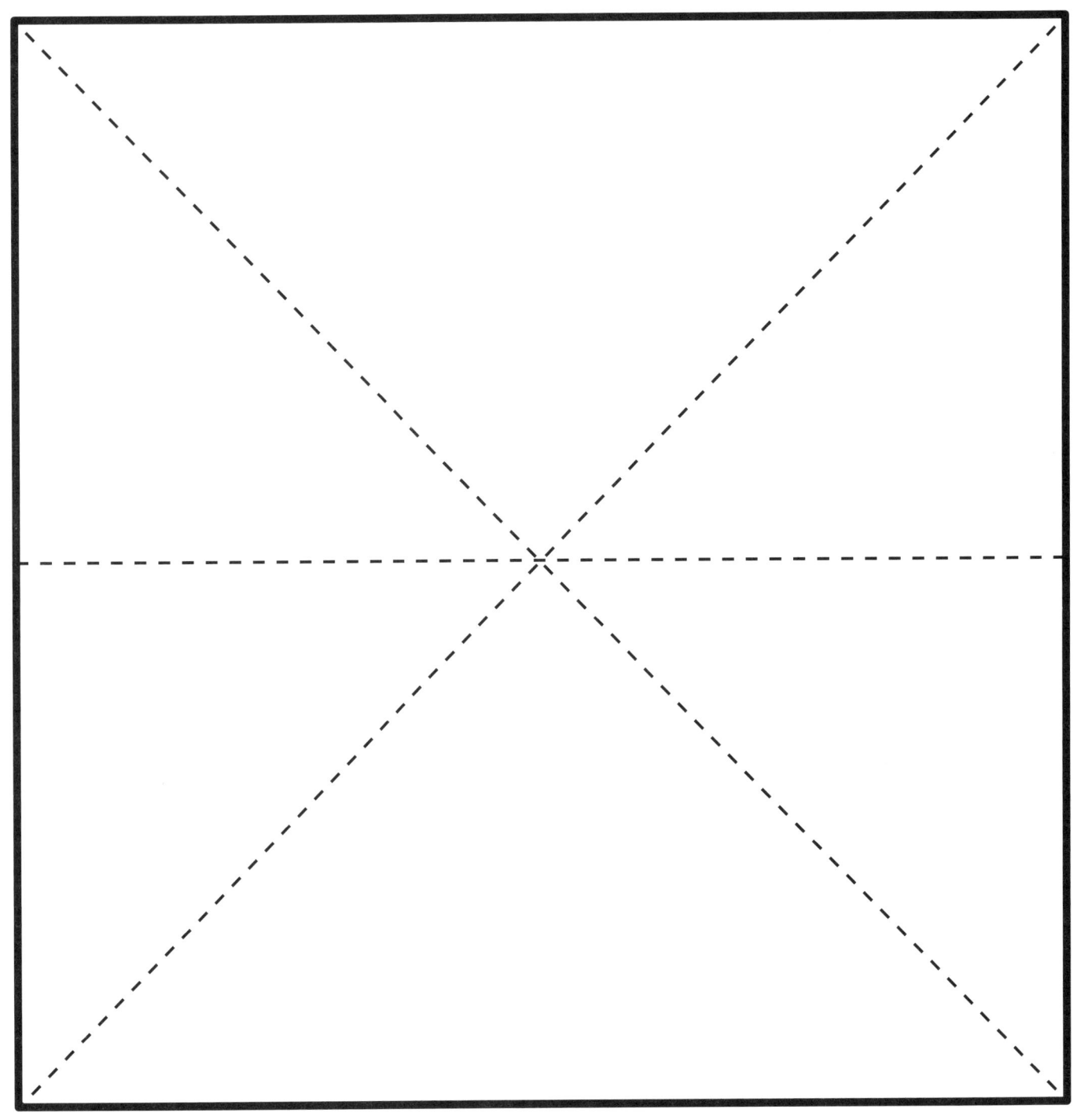

Puzzle Pieces

Cut out each puzzle along the solid lines to create a three- or four-piece puzzle. Apply glue to the back of each puzzle piece to attach it to a notebook page. Alternately, apply glue only to one edge of each piece to create flaps.

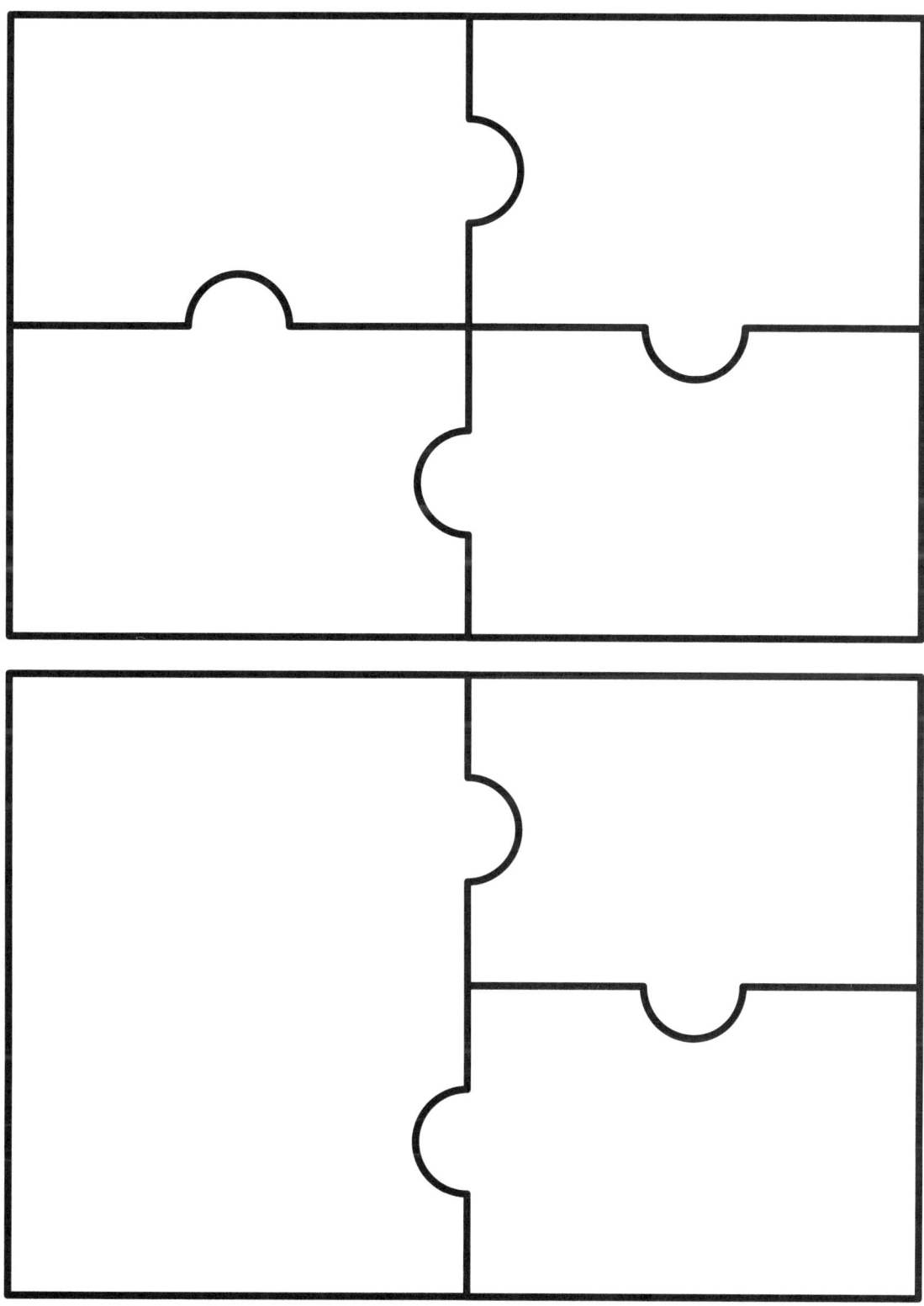

Flip Book

Cut out the two rectangular pieces on the solid lines. Fold each rectangle on the dashed lines. Fold the first piece so the gray glue section is inside the fold. Apply glue to the gray glue section and place the other folded rectangle on top so that the folds are nested and create a book with four cascading flaps. Make sure that the inside pages are facing up so that the edges of both pages are visible. Apply glue to the back of the book to attach it to a notebook page.

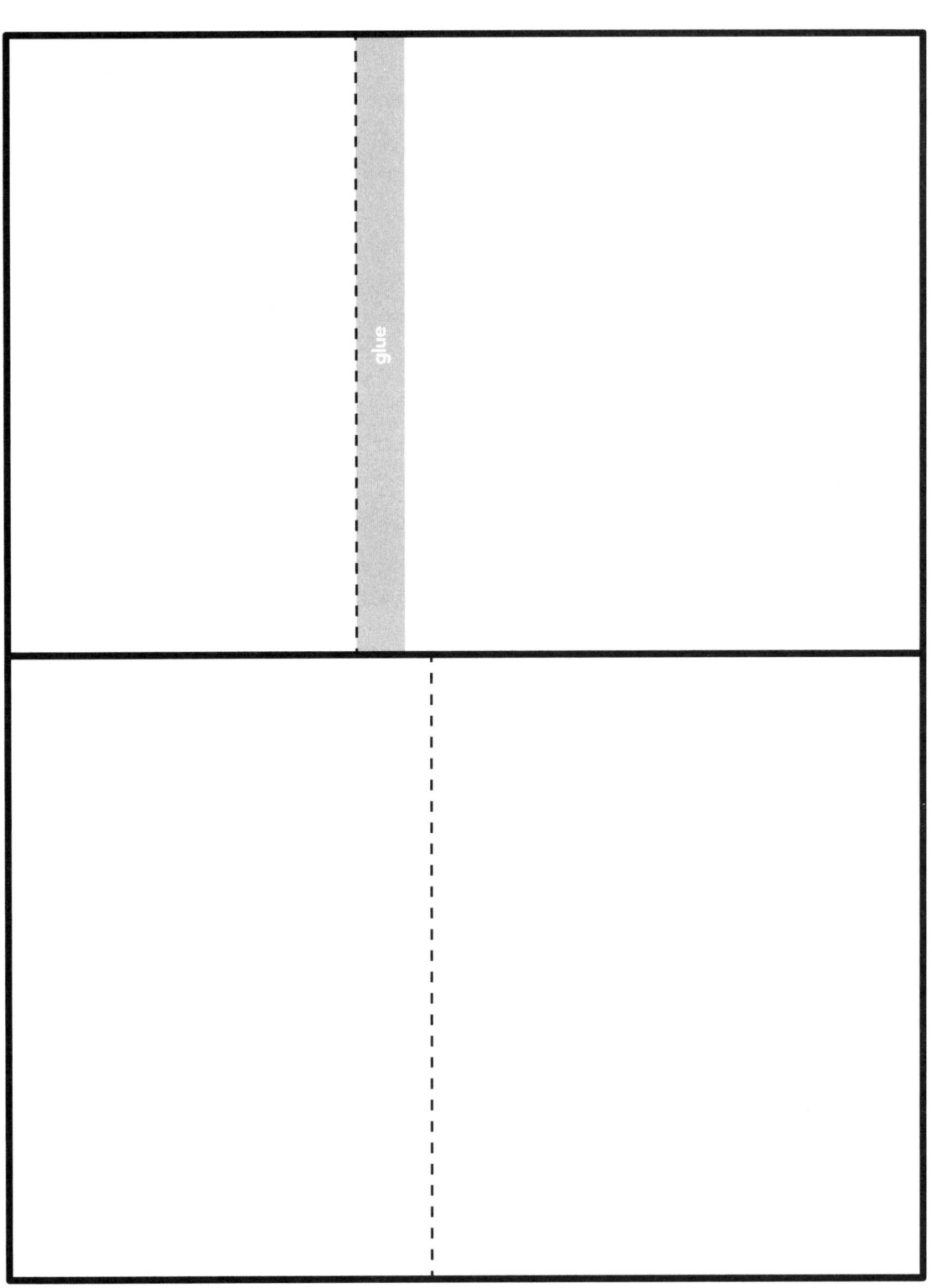